Independence in
Latin America

STUDIES IN WORLD CIVILIZATION

Independence in Latin America

A Comparative Approach

SECOND EDITION

Richard Graham
University of Texas at Austin

McGraw-Hill, Inc.
New York   St. Louis   San Francisco   Auckland   Bogotá   Caracas
Lisbon   London   Madrid   Mexico City   Milan   Montreal
New Delhi   San Juan   Singapore   Sydney   Tokyo   Toronto

INDEPENDENCE IN LATIN AMERICA
A Comparative Approach

6 7 8 9   BKM BKM   0 9 8 7 6 5 4 3 2 1

ISBN 0-07-024008-6

This book was set in Goudy Oldstyle by ComCom, Inc.
The editors were Pamela Gordon and Larry Goldberg;
the production supervisor was Paula Flores.
The cover was designed by Merrill Haber.

Cover Credit: The Battle of Carabobo, The Bettmann Archive.

PHOTO CREDITS: p. 32: The Bettmann Archive. pp. 59, 116 (left), 144: Jean Baptiste Debret, *Voyage pittoresque e historique au Brésil, ou Séjour d'un artiste français au Brésil* (Paris: Firmin Didot Fréres, Imprimeurs de l'Institut de France, 1834–39). p. 91: Courtesy Benson Latin American Collection, University of Texas at Austin. p. 97: Manuel Rivera Cambas, *Los Gobernantes de Mexico: Galeria de biografias y retratos* . . . (Mexico: Aguilar Ortiz, 1873), Vol. II. p. 115: Narcisse Edmond Joseph Desmadryl, *Galeria nacional: o, Colección de biografias e retratos de hombres celebres de Chile* . . . (Santiago: Impr. Chilena, 1854), Vol. I. p. 116 (right): Sebastião Augusto Sisson, *Galeria dos brasileiros illustres (os contemporaneos)* (Rio de Janeiro: Lith. de S. A. Sisson, 1861).

Library of Congress Cataloging-in-Publication Data

Graham, Richard, (date).
    Independence in Latin America: a comparative approach / Richard Graham. —2nd ed.
        p.   cm. —(Studies in world civilization)
    Includes bibliographical references (p.   ) and index.
    ISBN 0-07-024008-6
    1. Latin America—History—Wars of Independence, 1806–1830.
I. Title.   II. Series: Studies in world civilization (McGraw-Hill, Inc.)
F1412.G64   1994
980'.02—dc20   93-40045

To the Memory of My Father
and My Mother

Contents

Preface

Latin America is marked by its diversity. Only from the outsider's point of view does it seem a single unit. Yet there are sufficient commonalities within it to make comparisons valid, comparisons that can lead to insights as to the reasons for those diverse experiences. Comparative history has this power to focus attention on causative factors all too easily ignored in national histories. During a period of two decades beginning in 1808 most of Latin America became independent from Spain and Portugal, and this common experience had common roots; yet the course followed to that end differed markedly from one country to another. It is my purpose here to recount this story and highlight through comparisons some of the most important but easily ignored forces that shaped the course of these events.

There has been much vigorous scholarship on Latin America since the publication of the first edition of this book, and I have incorporated much of the new knowledge into this second edition. Both in Latin America and among North American historians research has been intense. Especially important is our growing, albeit still limited, knowledge of the social history of the epoch. Yet I have striven to be concise, sometimes sacrificing detail for the sake of the reader's patience and pocketbook.

Latin American history is part of a larger story, certainly a chapter in the development of "Western" civilization. Although the primary focus of this book is Latin America, I have also paid some attention to the European context, especially to the rise of industrial capitalism and the resulting European drive to expand its reach. Although practically every European history textbook refers to the "expansion of Europe," it is perhaps not the era of discovery and conquest that best exemplifies that process; for it was precisely when the political control of overseas colonies weakened and seemed to disappear that the process of European expansion was most intense.

Special thanks are due to my students, on whom I tried out several of these ideas and from whom I gathered many. My colleague Standish Meacham looked over some portions of the text dealing with European events. Both advice and ideas were sometimes ignored, so the end result is entirely my responsibility.

McGraw-Hill and I would like to thank the following reviewers for their many helpful comments and suggestions: Vincent de Baca, University of San Diego; Roberta Delson, United States Merchant Marine Academy; Dan Lewis, University of California at Santa Barbara; Wayne Osborn, Iowa State University; and Pedro Santoni, California State University at San Bernardino.

RICHARD GRAHAM

Chapter One
Colonies in Flux

Three factors delimited the course and ultimately shaped the meaning of Latin American independence movements: First, the beginnings of a world economic system centered in northern (or northwestern) Europe, rooted in capitalism, and accompanied by a new ideology encompassing individual freedom, democratic government, and a scientific approach to the natural and social world; second, the interests of colonial elites, who in varying degrees supported or opposed independence and sought to maintain control of the lower classes; finally, the pressure of these working classes, which, sometimes successfully, sometimes not, sought to defend themselves in the face of worsening economic conditions and altered political realities. The rise of capitalism in northern Europe, a long process which had been stimulated in part by New World wealth during the sixteenth and seventeenth centuries, created a growing eighteenth-century demand for raw materials and luxuries from the Portuguese and Spanish colonies. Colonial landowners, ranchers, and miners increasingly desired to supply these "colonial" goods directly to the consuming centers rather than through Spain or Portugal and to import manufactured goods on the same basis. But to produce those goods they often relied on unfree labor, and, in order to control the workers, masters felt the need for the political stability and governmental authority that Spain and Portugal could supply. That is, the spread of a single world economy tended to stimulate many members of the elite to seek independence, whereas social tension in the colonies often braked that impulse. The ideas that accompanied the growing economic connections with northern Europe were held by only a small number of leaders in Portuguese and Spanish America; but this group proved influential because it was linked to the economically powerful and—once independence was secured—to the politically powerful as well. These factors were not the "causes" of independence, as we shall see in Chapter 3, but they set the contours and directed the outcomes of, and gave meaning to, the portentous events examined in this book.

To speak of independence requires an understanding of what it meant to be a colony. There have been many types of colonies in the history of the world; but in the seventeenth and eighteenth centuries one of the predominant types was characterized most of all by a trade monopoly. That is, the merchants of the metropolis—or rather a subset of these—secured from their respective governments the exclusive right to trade with the colony. To secure this monopoly against competitors from other countries or from the colony itself, the political power and authority of the metropolis had to be maintained. Navies had to protect the coast, military force had to be organized, navigation acts passed, customs offices set up, governors appointed, and courts established. To pay for all this, governments levied taxes. Efforts by colonials to produce goods that could be supplied from Europe were viewed with alarm and often forbidden. And if colonial products were to be shipped in sufficient quantities to make the trade worthwhile, workers who would otherwise have preferred to enter the wilderness and produce their own food had to be compelled to produce tobacco, cotton, sugar, cacao, or coffee and labor in mines to bring up gold, silver, or diamonds. Evidently those areas of the New World where soils or climate led only to the production of crops like wheat or barley, which Europe supplied for itself, can be considered a different type of colony. As well, cattle-raising regions managed to produce hides and other pastoral products for export without the need for the compulsion of workers because in this case labor needs were low. But in the remaining regions one finds a mass of unfree, or at any rate compelled, laborers dominated by a wealthy stratum of local proprietors. Alongside the latter were agents of privileged European merchant houses engaged in overseas trade and an imposing list of bureaucrats directed by the metropolis. In Spanish America an elaborate Church hierarchy served to legitimize the entire system.

Implicit in this colonial structure were three sources of tension: that between workers and the propertied; that between the producers of exports and the monopoly merchants; and that between the merchant communities of the respective mother countries, each of which would wish to maintain its own monopoly while raiding the colonies of others. One overriding question by the end of the eighteenth century was whether the colonial elites could free themselves from metropolitan control without endangering their own dominance over the workers. As Simon Bolívar later put it, "A great volcano lies at our feet. Who shall restrain the oppressed classes?"[1]

In the remainder of this chapter it is my purpose to address these points from various perspectives, keeping the focus on how the eighteenth century was a time of particularly intense change. The rise of England as the center of the new capitalistic order had particular implications for the eighteenth-century Spanish and Portuguese empires, but changes for colonial elites were also brought on by alterations in the imperial structures of power. If anything, these changes focused ever more attention on the central issue of trade monopolies. Meanwhile, the century also witnessed a significant shift in patterns of agricultural production, with important implications for the workers, and the tensions and frictions that separated the various strata in Spanish and Portuguese societies became more intense. As well, the power of the Church to vouchsafe the authority of the state lessened, while the competing ideological role of the European Enlightenment grew. Finally, I return to Bolívar's question, as it is especially relevant in considering the Haitian Revolution.

The Rise of England

In the long, competitive struggle among the merchants of Spain, Portugal, France, Holland, and England, the first two gradually lost ground. Portugal's and Spain's inability to keep up resulted from their

---

[1] Quoted in John Lynch, *The Spanish American Revolutions, 1808–1826* (New York: Norton, 1973), p. 23.

failure to share the transformations in social relationships that were occurring in these other countries. Especially in England, new property relationships and new labor arrangements gradually transformed the economy and society from about 1500. In place of nobles and peasants bound by ancient, customary ties, landowning entrepreneurs—the gentry and yeomen farmers—increasingly hired wage workers to produce agricultural products or wool. Meanwhile, a process of legally enclosing the peasant common lands slowly transferred more and more of them to private hands, and many peasants lost the control they had earlier exercised over the soil they tilled. They then had no alternative but to seek employment for wages in either rural or urban occupations. Merchants prospered from the exchange of the expanding supply of goods from the countryside and in turn financed the production of woolen textiles. The entrepreneurial classes, both rural and urban, accumulated more and more of the surplus from production, and individual success encouraged those who sought to gain from private investment. The new set of relationships released enormous human energy.

In the seventeenth century, these newly prosperous groups in England secured sufficient power to wrest a large measure of state control from the nobility, most particularly through the English or Puritan Revolution, a violent civil war that culminated in the victory of Oliver Cromwell and the beheading of Charles I in 1649. The government then became more than ever interested in protecting and expanding overseas opportunities for the commercial classes. Jamaica was seized from Spain in 1655, not only to place a sugar-producing island within British hands but to provide a base for an extensive smuggling commerce to the Spanish mainland. By the same token, Parliament passed laws to ensure that Jamaican sugar and Virginian tobacco could be transported only on ships belonging to English businessmen; that these and other enumerated articles could be shipped only to England; and that colonists' importing manufactured goods from anywhere but England was forbidden. Meanwhile, wars against the Dutch helped secure expanding trade opportunities elsewhere. Treaties (called the "unequal treaties") were imposed by force upon the Portuguese according to the provisions of which British merchants in Portugal (from 1642) would be judged by English judges according to English commercial law and be allowed (from 1654) to trade directly with Brazil. Later a limited number of English businessmen even gained the treaty right to set up shop in Brazil itself. After the "Glorious Revolution" of 1688 in England, these steps on behalf of the business class proved irreversible. Finally, at the conclusion of the War of the Spanish Succession (1700–1713) Spain had to cede to British merchants the monopoly right to supply slaves to its empire as well as to send one ship a year to trade at an annual fair in Panamá. At every step state power was used to advance the commercial interests of British merchants overseas.

During this same long period of transition to capitalism, British thinkers hammered out a new set of ideas that presented a rationale for the new order. As one example we may take John Locke (1632–1704), whose view of human psychology—shaped, he believed, entirely by experience and not by one's noble or common birth—lay at the very heart of the new competitive economy and whose political argument set out the principal tenets of parliamentary democracy. His individualistic rationale would form the hallmark of the new economic and political system.

In the eighteenth century the newly dominant class pushed England into a still more dynamic experience, usually referred to as the Industrial Revolution. Although its true flowering came only in the nineteenth century, its eighteenth-century transformations meant that still more agricultural workers sought employment for wages in the cities, and steadily growing profits accrued to those who owned factories. Agricultural entrepreneurs fed industrialism and vice versa, aiding the accumulation of capital for investment. Cotton textile mills required a new raw material that had to come from overseas, and there was an increased demand for dyes such as indigo and cochineal. The new wealth and urban growth also stimulated the demand for "desserts" like tobacco, cacao, coffee, and sugar.

As well, the expanding production of textiles and other manufactured goods impelled a search for ever more consumers. The Spanish and Portuguese empires offered an obvious potential market, and British authorities officially ignored but unofficially encouraged smuggling and contraband trade into those colonies. Especially notorious was the subterfuge by which the right to send one five-hundred-ton ship off Panamá was abused: It unloaded goods during the daylight hours but was resupplied at night by other English ships, with the result that it stayed in port unloading for weeks and even months while local authorities looked the other way. By the end of the century a quarter of all British exports went to the West Indies, that is, principally to Spanish America.

The Spanish government responded to the plague of smugglers by mounting a coast guard which sometimes seized British ships on the high seas if they were suspected of smuggling. In 1739 a Captain Jenkins, commanding a British ship boarded by the Spanish, lost his ear in the ensuing fracas, and this event led to an outright war (the War of Jenkins' Ear) that, merging with the War of the Austrian Succession, only ended in 1748. The Seven Years' War (1756–1763), also known as the French and Indian War, was largely a struggle over overseas empires. As Spain sided with France, the English took the opportunity to capture Havana (1762) and make it an entrepôt for British merchants. The Spanish retaliated by seizing Colonia do Sacramento (in present-day Uruguay) from England's ally Portugal, which had been using it as a base for an extensive smuggling ring whereby Peruvian silver was exchanged for European goods and African slaves. At the end of the war the Spanish returned this town to the Portuguese and the English gave up Havana in exchange for Florida. The Spanish conceded to the British the right to send dyewood cutters to the coast of Central America and to maintain settlements there, although these would formally be under Spanish sovereignty.

The year 1776 brought permanent changes in colonial relationships. Before that date the British would hardly have openly advocated the end of colonial monopolies, for they themselves held a major colony and sought to maintain exclusive rights to trade with it. But once the United States declared its independence and then succeeded in winning it, little could restrain the British. In fact, even in 1766 Jamaica had been declared a free port, open to foreign ships, since British industrialists were now more interested in selling their products and buying raw materials than in protecting the trade of their erstwhile allies, the monopoly merchants. Meanwhile, British theoreticians had been rethinking the mercantilist philosophy. In 1776 Adam Smith (1723–1790) published his *Inquiry into the Nature and Causes of the Wealth of Nations*, arguing (among other things) that the maintenance of colonies for the exclusive trade of monopoly merchants made no sense. The British were thus freed practically and intellectually from any restraint in attempting to end the colonial monopolies of Spain and Portugal.

Meanwhile, no economic and social changes of similar scope occurred in Spain or Portugal. No seventeenth-century English Revolution occurred there. The nobility continued to enjoy the deferential service of peasants; the land was still tilled in customary ways, and few held land solely to make a profit from it rather than as a way to enhance their social status; no large class of landed businessmen accumulated capital for industrial investment; and no great surplus of labor was driven off the land to seek wages in the cities. Aside from some industries in northeastern Spain which prospered in the late eighteenth century, the country remained predominantly agricultural. Great merchant houses enjoyed the monopoly of colonial trade but, on the whole, did not invest their profits in industry. Instead, they increasingly bought manufactured goods from northern Europe and shipped colonial goods there in exchange. The state protected these merchants but was not dominated by them. The dynamism of the capitalistic wage economy passed these countries by. With a lagging economy went sagging government revenues, making it all the more difficult to protect the far-flung empires established in the sixteenth century. So while British merchants sought new markets and new sources of supply for an expanding industrial complex, Spain and Portugal were increasingly unable to withstand their onslaught.

At the same time the Iberian powers were ever more self-consciously committed to maintaining the colonial monopoly of trade. These views found expression in many treatises, but can be exemplified here by the words of two administrators sent out to rule the colonies. The viceroy of Peru, responding in 1812 to Creole complaints about limits and restrictions on trade, noted that freedom of trade "would be tantamount to decreeing the separation of these Dominions from the Mother country since, once direct trade with foreigners [is] established . . . the fate of European Spain would matter little to them."[2] A governor in Salvador, Brazil, responding to the town council's request for fewer controls on commerce, put it this way in 1807:

> If I were to embrace slickly written arguments deduced from arbitrary principles, I would say along with modern economists that any brake or restriction is prejudicial to the freedom of commerce, even colonial commerce. But I cannot help believing the opposite, knowing that

---

[2] Quoted in J. R. Fisher, *Government and Society in Colonial Peru: The Intendant System, 1784–1814* (London: Athlone, 1970), p. 154.

colonial establishments like this one have as their primary purpose (or truly their only one) the welfare and utility of the Metropolis, to which colonies should remain directly dependent, . . . trading with it exclusively.[3]

To maintain such a monopoly required an elaborate political apparatus.

Ruler and Ruled

The military, diplomatic, and political fate of the Iberian peninsula during the eighteenth century had major repercussions for the structures of government in Latin America. As noted, the century began with the War of the Spanish Succession. Louis XIV of France had decided to enforce his family's claim to the throne of Spain and hoped eventually to unite the two kingdoms, but other powers objected. In the end France and Spain remained forever separate, but a major branch of the Bourbon line did replace the Hapsburg dynasty on the throne of Spain. The first three Bourbon kings, Philip V (reigned 1700–1746), Ferdinand VI (1746–1759), and Charles III (1759–1788), inspired by the example of their French cousins and at first surrounded by French advisers, set to work to transform Spain; in so doing they wrought major changes upon Spanish America as well.

Perhaps the most important alterations made by the Bourbons were the result of their view of the relationship between king and subject. The Hapsburgs had thought of themselves as patriarchs who occupied their position not because of the divine right of kings but, so to speak, because of the divine right of fathers. According to the Hapsburg view, God had ordained the family as the basic unit of society, and the family was hierarchically structured with the father at its head; the king was also the head of a similarly structured "family" with every member of society occupying a place within it fixed by God. This basic political philosophy, which permeated the entire social organism, elicited and depended upon relationships of authority-de-

---

[3] Governor of Bahia to Visconde de Anadia, Salvador, 27 Aug. 1807, Arquivo Histórico Ultramarino, Lisbon, Cat. 29.985.

pendence and benevolence-loyalty. No legislation could change the deeply meaningful link between king and subject, just as no law could alter the biological connection between father and child. Legal theorists in the sixteenth century had clearly laid out the responsibilities of the king toward his subjects. The Bourbons, however, thought somewhat differently about the relationship between king and subject. Although not entirely free of such a familial viewpoint, the Bourbons were more apt to think of the king as a ruler than as a father and to judge him by the effectiveness of his rule rather than by his love for his subjects. Many Spanish Americans clung to the Hapsburg image of the patriarchal state and resisted the Bourbons' new political philosophy. The long process through which people in England or France came to direct their loyalty toward an abstract state rather than toward a monarch personally had not yet begun even in Spain and Portugal, much less in Spanish and Portuguese America. This failure to shift the locus of loyalty would have long-lasting repercussions.

Furthermore, Spanish Americans thought of themselves as legally linked to Spain merely by their king. At the time of the fifteenth-century discovery of America, Spain had consisted of two distinct kingdoms, albeit united by a common throne, and each kingdom had its own traditional institutions, courts, and councils to advise the king on local affairs. Subsequently there were also separate institutions for the kingdoms of Naples, the Netherlands, and (from 1580 to 1640, when the Spanish king claimed its throne) Portugal, despite the fact that they all shared the same ruler. The overseas empire was yet another kingdom with a separate council, known as the Council of the Indies, to advise the king on American matters. Under the Hapsburgs the Council of the Indies was the highest administrative, legislative, and judicial body that the Spanish Americans dealt with before appealing to the king. So Spanish Americans did not consider themselves colonials of Spain. When superimposed upon the patriarchal view of the state, this self-image became more than a legalistic question. These kingdoms were like distinct families with the same father; and if the father were to be removed, nothing would make one family subordinate to the other. In contrast, the Bourbons conceived of all Spanish territory as a single kingdom and believed that the purpose of the Spanish-American colonies was to advance the interests of Spain. In this view they were supported by most political leaders in eighteenth-century Spain.

The Bourbons put a high value upon efficiency. Scientific administration was, in theory at least, the keystone of their approach. Direct lines of command, the ability to pinpoint responsibility, clear separation of jurisdictions, and specialized functions were the goals of the reforms the Bourbons imposed upon Spain and Spanish America. The Bourbons' first step toward change was to create a cabinet which met to consider the affairs of the entire realm, whether in Aragon or in Spanish America. Then, impelled by the same logic, they broke up the affairs of the empire into component parts: for instance, military affairs were handled by the Minister of War while relations with other colonial powers were assigned to the Minister of Foreign Affairs. The Council of the Indies dwindled in importance.

The Bourbon kings noted that if American affairs were to foster the welfare of Spain, the economic life of Spanish America would have to be revitalized, especially given Spain's frequent wars. Indeed, according to the "Family Compact" drawn up through a series of treaties between the king of Spain and his cousin the king of France, they determined that their common interests depended upon changes in American administration. One such change was the naming of intendants for Spanish America. Intendants, used first in France and then in Spain, were administrative officers who had as their principal objective the increase of royal revenue by stimulating the local economy and enforcing the collection of taxes. As idealized, the system of intendants was a perfect example of the Bourbons' belief in efficient, centralized administration. Its application in all of Spanish America by 1786 meant the end of a complicated and extremely subdivided political system in which the viceroy had exerted his power through a large number of provincial officials of different ranks and titles. The old scheme was now replaced by a simplified structure of authority in which a relatively few intendants reported directly to the viceroy on some matters and directly to the king on matters of finance.

The Bourbons actually took vast areas completely out of the control of the two viceroys, who had until then ruled all Spanish America from their seats in Mexico City and Lima. In 1717 the crown set up the Viceroyalty of New Granada (see map on back cover), encompassing the territory now included in Venezuela, Colombia, and Ecuador,[4] with its seat in Bogotá. In 1776 the Bourbons established the Viceroyalty of Río de la Plata, stripping from the Viceroyalty of Peru most of the territory now included in Bolivia, Argentina, Paraguay, and Uruguay. Then they created two captaincies-general (virtually viceroyalties, but without as much prestige) for what are now Chile and Venezuela.

The Bourbons also realized that they had to pay closer attention to the Viceroyalty of New Spain, the territory that is now Mexico, Central America, and much of the southwestern United States. Its northern frontier was threatened by the Russians, the French, and the British, as well as by Indian tribes being squeezed southward. But it was patently ridiculous to think of setting up a viceroyalty with all its accompanying pomp and ceremony in this sparsely settled region, where the largest town had a population of some 2,500. So in 1776 the area that today forms the northern states of Mexico and the southwestern ones in the United States was taken out of the jurisdiction of the viceroy in Mexico City and placed under a military commandant-general.

The viceroys, under both the Hapsburgs and the Bourbons, were advised by *audiencias*, a kind of miniature Council of the Indies that, like it, also acted as a court. Under the Bourbons the appointees to audiencias tended to be almost exclusively Spanish-born, reversing the trend under the Hapsburgs and thus enhancing royal control but lessening the influence of the locally well-off. So Spaniards in Europe, unlike those born in America, came to think of the overseas kingdom as their American colony, not as a separate kingdom.

Spaniards born in America ("Creoles") did still exercise a vestige of governmental responsibility in the *cabildos* (sometimes called *ayuntamientos*), councils charged with local government. Their jurisdiction included both rural and urban areas and sometimes extended for hundreds of miles; their focus, however, was always a central city or town. The cabildos had gradually lost much of their actual power, however, because an increasing number of petty details were covered by laws issued from Madrid. Furthermore, as the crown became more

---

[4] For the sake of simplicity all areas are henceforth referred to by their modern names.

desperate for money, it often sold, sometimes in perpetuity, the seats on the cabildo; therefore, few people looked to the cabildo as a source of vitality or new ideas. But it was the only local government authority, and it remained important as a symbol, as the place where "the people" found representation. The intendants sent out by the Bourbon kings in the eighteenth century often gave cabildos new life by their reforms, even though these officials were intended to supply a new intermediary focus of loyalty; the cabildos remained a recourse in time of trouble. Clashes between locally oriented cabildos and the Spanish-dominated audiencias became commonplace, especially as independence approached.

In Brazil local government remained stronger than in Spanish America. From the beginning it had received less attention from Lisbon than Spanish America from Madrid. The real empire of Portugal in the early sixteenth century had been India and the spice islands in southeast Asia. Brazil, with no precious minerals discovered until the beginning of the eighteenth century, had been only a second thought, and the Portuguese paid scant attention to it unless it was threatened by other nations. So Portuguese Americans were practically left to govern themselves. The basic unit of government— beyond the sugar plantation or cattle ranch itself—was the *senado da câmara*, or *câmara* for short, an elective city/county council. The câmaras were usually dominated by planters, who, in contrast to their Spanish counterparts in the cabildo, could wield real power through it either because the câmaras were too far from Portugal to be effectively controlled or because they had been granted rights, privileges, and exemptions by careless Portuguese kings.

The reforming zeal of the Bourbons was echoed and many times anticipated in Portugal by the king's chief minister from 1750 to 1777, Sebastião José de Carvalho e Melo, who eventually received the title of Marquis of Pombal. He may be considered the "enlightened despot" of Portugal like Charles III of Spain, Frederick the Great of Prussia, or Joseph II of Austria, eighteenth-century rulers who combined absolutism with forceful economic and religious reforms. Pombal could be frightfully cruel and imprisoned many political opponents, but he also won a great deal of respect for his reforming zeal and great energy. He reorganized public services, placed colonial affairs firmly in the hands of the minister of the Navy and Overseas Territories, and streamlined colonial government. He consolidated in royal hands the last of the proprietary colonies created in sixteenth-century Brazil. He enhanced the authority of the viceroy over the governors and captains-general in all the provinces of Brazil and in 1763 moved the seat of the viceroyalty from Salvador to the now prospering Rio de Janeiro. He worked to lessen the power of the câmaras. But unlike the Bourbons, Pombal recognized the value of incorporating Portuguese men born in Brazil into the imperial machine. As Brazil had no university, planters' sons received their higher education at the University of Coimbra, so Pombal did not have far to go to find capable Brazilians trained in Roman law and the principle of centralized authority. These he placed in many administrative posts in India, Africa, and Brazil. Pombal's legacy was a strengthened empire.

Both Charles III and Pombal sought to raise revenues from the colonies by reforming taxation. The long-established sales tax in Spanish America was raised from 4 to 6 percent and its collection placed directly under royal appointees, rather than farmed out to private bidders. The intendants were given particular responsibility for seeing that tax collection went well, and they reported on these matters directly to the king rather than to the viceroy. Pombal established a new, centralized treasury department in Portugal under his personal direction and paid close attention to colonial revenues. The mining economy of Minas Gerais, in interior Brazil, was notorious for its tax evasion schemes, so one of Pombal's successors, lacking his political skill, in 1788 decreed a per capita tax to make up for alleged arrears in public revenues. In both Portuguese and Spanish America (as in English America) protest and even rebellion resulted from these new tax policies. In Peru riots broke out in 1780, opening the way for an Indian uprising; in Colombia the next year an armed revolt of tradesmen and artisans was principally driven by resistance to the new imposts; and in Ouro Preto authorities uncovered a conspiracy in 1789, led by those who owed the most in back taxes, that purposed complete independence from Portugal. It had become increasingly obvious that taxes did not benefit the colonials, and the same was true for the restrictions laid on colonial trade.

Trade

Before the eighteenth century all Spanish-controlled transatlantic trade centered on four ports: Cádiz in Spain and Cartagena, Panamá, and Veracruz in America. The practical necessity of protecting silver-laden ships from hostile pirates led to the use of fleets guarded by men-of-war. The ships to and from Spain, therefore, were required to leave port together and were not allowed to separate until they were safely at or near their destination. The result was, for example, that manufactured goods produced in England to be consumed in Buenos Aires went first to Spain and then to Panamá, next by sea to Lima along the relatively safe Pacific coast, and then overland across the towering mountains and broad plains to Argentina. In Spain only Cádiz was permitted to participate, for its merchant guild held great political power and was the first on the commercial scene. And in each of the entrepôts through which their goods passed, other merchants, usually the agents for the Cádiz monopolists and even family members, maintained a tight hold on the profitable interchange. If Spain had produced the goods, it might have been able to maintain this commercial system indefinitely, but this was not the case; as we have seen, smuggling became the bane of royal administrators in the Americas. Sometimes through war and sometimes through subterfuge, the English managed to invade the American markets, exchanging cottons and knives for cacao, sugar, and hides, not to mention bullion. During the first part of the eighteenth century smuggling increased rapidly. Non-Spanish masters had the daring; the Spanish Americans, especially those outside the monopoly ports, had the desire for cheaper goods; and Spanish officials often connived to make this a widespread practice.

The Bourbons set to work to reform and modernize the commercial system. First, they liberalized the regulations, making it easier and cheaper to trade legally through Spain. Second, they created monopoly companies modeled on the Dutch or British East India Companies in which capitalists from other parts of Spain besides Cádiz could participate. These companies were assigned special areas in the Americas as their preserve to defend and develop. Finally, a steadily increasing number of ports were allowed to trade with one another and the fleet system was ultimately abandoned. The culmination of this policy was the so-called Decree of Free Trade (1778), which allowed twenty-four ports in America to trade with almost any port in Spain. Commerce was still limited to Spanish subjects and in effect still fell into the hands of the great Spanish merchants, who had the necessary capital; in fact, by sanctioning the establishment of new merchant guilds outside Mexico City and Lima, the control exercised by Spanish-born merchants increased. Also, by curtailing smuggling, these measures further intensified the exclusive claim of Spanish merchants upon the trade of the colony. But the decree was a great boon to ports like Buenos Aires that had previously suffered most from the old restrictions.

The Portuguese had never centralized trade in Lisbon, so it was really impossible to maintain an efficient fleet system. Also, the main product of Brazil was sugar, a relatively bulky product compared to bullion and also perishable; only at times of war did the Portuguese require the ships to sail together under escort and even then with limited success and much grumbling from the shippers. When Portugal was ruled by Spanish kings between 1580 and 1640 the Hapsburgs had despaired in their efforts to impose what they considered an orderly commercial system upon it. Trade was always carried on directly with Portugal from every Brazilian port, and even foreign ships were occasionally given legal permission to trade there, not to mention the selected British merchants whose rights had been secured through the "unequal treaties." Pombal did create monopoly companies to foster the development of the northernmost coastal regions of Brazil, and they had a limited but noticeable success, especially in fostering cotton cultivation. And he took up an old plan to lessen the deleterious effect of the Inquisition upon "New Christian" (that is, descendants of Jews forcibly converted to Christianity in the late fifteenth century) businessmen in Portugal. But the real stimulus to Brazilian commerce came from the expanding markets of northern Europe and, eventually, from economic disruptions in the French and Spanish colonies.

Hacienda and Plantation

A dominant feature of the land tenure pattern in Latin America by the eighteenth century was the large landed estate. A basic value among the upper classes of Spain and Portugal, probably inculcated in childhood, was that land was the most legitimate symbol of status. The origins of this attitude lay deep in the Iberian past, and it was bolstered by legal devices such as the entailed estate, which made it impossible to divide up certain properties at the death of the owner.

When the sixteenth-century conquistadors arrived in the highlands of Mexico and Peru, they found millions of Indians accustomed to a master-man relationship, prepared to labor on land that was not individually theirs, and able to carry on agricultural activity without much supervision; thus it was only natural that the first Spaniards should secure large estates for themselves. The Portuguese found no such population and turned instead to Africa for a supply of slave labor that would enable them to produce sugar; the king made enormous land grants to those who could prove they had the wherewithal to turn them into plantations. For one reason or another a great deal of the tillable land of Latin America was divided among a relatively few men.

In considering the position of these colonial elites, however, it is useful to draw a distinction between those who held land primarily for the sake of the status it conferred and those who looked upon its ownership as an investment like any other, to be used to make a profit. Evidently the distinction should not be exaggerated, for income from land was universally desired. But the *principal* aim could differ. I shall here call the estates of the first group "haciendas" and those of the second group "plantations," even though these words and others were used sometimes interchangeably and certainly with great variation across the continents of America.

Keeping these qualifications in mind, it is then meaningful to describe the hacienda as a property held mainly for its status-contributing value and not primarily for profit. The produce of the hacienda went to feed the workers, to supply the owner's town-house kitchen, and to be exchanged in barter for the luxuries required for urban living. But otherwise the owner was not particularly concerned with its productivity: Sufficient profit, not maximum profit, was his goal. The workers, who had moved onto hacienda lands from their villages, were paid in the limited right to use small plots of land for themselves and in credit at the company store. Because these store goods were advanced at prices that could not possibly be met by the workers, a system of debt peonage resulted. The system was perpetual since both custom and law made it impossible to seek other employment until the debt had been repaid. The result was that the peon, or debt slave, grew up on the hacienda, inherited his father's debt, and passed it on, considerably augmented, to his son.

In terms of the ideals that were voiced at the time, the system was characterized by mutuality and consent. The imagined paternalism of the Hapsburg kings was matched by that of the *hacendado*, or owner, who supposedly thought of his peons as his children. It was his duty to see that the peons were treated when they were sick, to get them out of jail after a drunken Saturday-night brawl, and to provide an occasional visit by a priest to take care of their spiritual needs. He would have been shocked had he been called an exploiter. The peons, in turn, were supposed and expected to be loyal and loving. On the owner's birthday, they would shower him with gifts. It was all imagined as a family, and its familial character was reinforced by the actual system of *compadrazgo*: the owner became the godfather of the peon's children and thus assumed, through ritual, the position of close relative. In this and in other ways the owner became the surrogate of the king and even of God. Unfortunately for his "children," like God and king the owner did not often choose to live on the hacienda. He much preferred town life and left the administration of his estate in the hands of the *mayordomo*, whose sense of responsibility was only to the hacendado, never to the peon.

The hacienda was only very indirectly touched by the international economy. The primary exports from Spanish America had long been gold and silver, and European demands were linked to the agricultural activity on the hacienda only by the demand for foodstuffs to feed the workers in the mines or the inhabitants of the cities whose sophisticated culture the mines financed.

During the eighteenth century a new institution became increasingly prominent: the plantation. Changing economic needs in Europe account for its rise. As we have noted, the affluence of the European urban class created a market for tropical luxuries, such as sugar and tobacco, while cotton, cattle hides, and tallow were needed to supply expanding European industries. Added to these new demands was the local stimulus to search for new products as a financial substitute for silver and gold where ores of the best quality had been exhausted. Plantations, as defined here, were operated primarily for profit and not owned merely to gain enhanced social status. They were not devoted to subsistence agriculture or to supplying the relatively inelastic demand of local towns; they were plugged into the expanding and dynamic European economy. In contrast to the many haciendas that still survived, the plantations were often owned by new arrivals from Spain who knew of the overseas demand, had contacts with international merchants, and possessed the enterprise and drive to establish new ventures, even at some risk.

The ancient ties of man to land were broken by the plantation. The centers of Indian population had been in the highland areas, but tropical exports were produced in the sparsely populated lowland regions. To cultivate them, either the Indians would have to be moved from the highlands or black slaves would have to be imported from Africa. Iberian peoples had been accustomed to African slave labor for centuries; they had used African slaves on the Atlantic islands (Madeira, the Canaries, and the Cape Verdes) before the discovery of America and had introduced them into the New World in the sixteenth century. With the expanding needs of the invigorated plantation economies, it was only natural that Spanish-American plantation owners looked with heightened interest for labor in Africa. Slave traders, especially the British, brought in an ever-increasing number of human cargoes. The Bourbons even issued a new slave code which stimulated the use of black slaves by abolishing the ancient slave-trade monopolies. Whether slaves or free Indians lured down from the mountains by cash wages, no one imagined that these workers on the plantations were inspired by loyalty toward their master; and he openly regarded them only as factors of production, the cost of which must be carefully balanced out against profits.

The new economic activities also implied a shift in the center of economic gravity away from the mining areas and toward new centers that had previously been on the frontiers. This fact is especially noticeable in Spanish South America: Lima in the west began to lose ground, while Caracas in the north and Buenos Aires in the south increased in importance. Mexico City managed to cash in on both the old and the new economic activity, but even in Mexico the coastal regions entered a period of new importance.

Brazil had always been dominated by sugar plantations worked by slaves. Curiously, however, Brazil became more interested in mines just as Spanish America was turning toward plantations. The mines discovered in the province of Minas Gerais near Ouro Preto at the end of the seventeenth century finally gave Brazil the wealth and importance it had previously lacked. Cities now flourished, and Brazilians had the leisure to engage in the arts for the first time. But the mines in Brazil (mostly placer mines) were worked by slave labor and not by salaried workers, as in Mexico, or draft labor from Indian villages, as in Peru. And Brazilian sugar planters still dominated most urban centers and kept their eyes firmly on European markets. Certainly both planters and miners in Brazil viewed their activities as devoted to making a profit.

Hierarchy and Power

The Hapsburg political and economic system had been reinforced by the traditional structure of society in which everyone had a fixed position within a multilayered set of social categories. Each corporation—guild, religious order, or military rank—had its special rights and privileges. The guild system is an example. The goldsmiths and the shoemakers were each organized as if they formed a family in which the journeymen, as virtual children, were in a fixed relationship to the masters. Each guild had its particular identifying clothes, its own patron saint, its own section of town, and its own court where masters passed judgment over cases involving conflicts between members of the guild and sometimes between themselves and members of less privileged corporations. Similarly, in Spanish America the stockmen had their own guild and court where large landowners judged the fate of alleged cattle rustlers; and commercial law was applied by the state-sanctioned merchant guild, dominated by the wealthy merchants who engaged in international trade. The rights to special courts, special clothes, special places in parades, and other honors were called, collectively, *fueros*. The judicial system, thus divided up by occupation and corporation, reflected the more general view of society. Instead of being formed by individuals protected in their rights and mobile in relationship to one another, society was made up of castes, ranks, and corporations layered one atop another or lying side by side. The individual had multiple identities and multiple loyalties without a truly all-encompassing one, except as a Christian (and marginally, as a subject of a king)—never as a citizen of a nation. In this the Iberians resembled the *ancien régime* in much of Europe before the French Revolution.

The position of the Bourbon kings with regard to this social hierarchy was ambiguous. In some ways the Bourbons worked to destroy it, but in other ways they bolstered it or at least came to terms with it; for instance, in their effort to revitalize the mining industry in

Mexico, the Bourbons created a guild for mine owners with special rights and privileges in order to encourage an occupation considered less prestigious than landowning. The mining guild was naturally granted its own court to adjudicate questions arising within mining legislation, and this seemed to fit the older corporate structure of society. But the guild also supervised the new school of mines in Mexico in which the latest scientific principles were taught and a rational attitude toward the world was inculcated; individual social mobility was its natural concomitant. Although the corporate structure of society remained relatively unchanged, class divisions may have intensified in the eighteenth century.

In much of the Spanish-American highlands Indian villages with common lands that were legally inalienable continued to be the most typical arrangement. In a sense they too had their fueros. They were legally corporate bodies and not merely collections of individuals, and each had its own cabildo and village elders who exercised justice. Many of these villages successfully perpetuated their culture and much of their religion. Spanish law itself had long sought to prevent incursions by white colonists. The Bourbons even took some measures to alleviate the lot of Indian villages by forbidding the practice of forcing them to buy a certain amount of manufactured goods, a practice that had been effective in pushing Indians to seek employment for cash outside the village. Although not long enforced, this prohibition—along with many other royal decrees over the years—led many Indians to envision the king as their protector. Pombal, more so than the Bourbons, saw the Indians as potential subjects and desired their integration into Portuguese-speaking society as fast as possible. For one thing, he hoped to acquire legal claims to the Brazilian hinterland by designating as Portuguese the Indians who inhabited it. Although he forbade the enslavement of Indians, he forced religious orders to cease proffering them protection. And, as we have seen, in Spanish America generally the lot of Indians noticeably worsened on the plantations, and the eighteenth century was a sad time for them.

At the other extreme of the social spectrum were the Creoles, persons of Spanish descent born in America. They occupied many rungs of society, but, along with some Spaniards born in Spain (the "peninsulars"), they monopolized the most prestigious social positions, shutting out the Indians and mestizos (persons of mixed Indian-

Spanish descent). The great landowners and miners formed an aristocracy that was acutely class-conscious and liked to lord it over other groups, but they were often looked down upon by the peninsular Spaniards, despite the facts that many of them were only one generation removed from Spanish birth and their daughters often married new Spanish immigrants. Even the many peninsulars who had occupied lowly positions in Spain and began in America as peddlers, small shopkeepers, or artisans found their upward mobility eased by the solidarity of others born in Spain. One of the claims of the Spanish-born was that Creoles were naturally inferior, that is, that the American climate, or perhaps the American longitude, was somehow enervating. By nature, people born and raised in America, regardless of their parentage, were thought to lack intelligence, drive, and stamina. This idea is no more ridiculous than many of the prejudices that are still found among us today and was even accepted by many Creoles.

Between the Creoles and the Indians were the mestizos. It is sometimes estimated that only 600,000 Spaniards ever migrated to America; but, through racial mixture more than through outright force, they imposed their culture over a vast empire. The mestizos occupied a distinctly inferior social position and were accepted by neither the Indians nor the whites. Many mestizos were restless, ambitious, and anxious to prove that they were just as good as the whites. As a consequence they were often aggressive and resentful, for, despite their efforts, they did not frequently succeed. *Pardos*, that is, free mulattos (persons of mixed African and European descent), were even more discriminated against than mestizos and bore a number of legal disabilities. The Bourbons, however, revoked many of the laws that circumscribed their freedom.

People who were neither pure Spanish nor lived in Indian corporate communities were often labeled *castas*. A loose designation, the term included lower-class mestizos, pardos, blacks, black-Indian mixtures, and those Indians who had left the villages, spoke Spanish, and had culturally adapted. These distinctions among social groups were more economic and cultural than racial. Members of the castas were tried by separate courts, not allowed to carry personal weapons or own horses, exempted from certain taxes and from the tithe—since they paid the tribute or head tax instead—and restricted by sumptuary laws. Although most mestizos remained lowly, there were numerous examples of mestizos who, becoming wealthy, were able to buy their way into the white world for themselves or their descendants and be accepted in society as whites. For that matter, many of the best families were descended from conquistadors who had married into the Indian nobility. On the other hand, the mestizos' very ability to compete with the Creoles intensified the prejudice against them. During the eighteenth century it may well be that racist feeling was on the increase in Spanish America.

Creoles, especially those who lacked great wealth, resented the fact that the peninsular bureaucrats sent out by the Bourbon kings seemed to be more concerned with place of birth than with race. Perhaps the saving grace of the Spanish colonial system was that the Creoles did not monopolize all political power. They could amass great fortunes, operate huge estates, and hold all other American groups in contempt, but they could not run the government entirely in their own behalf, for the Spanish occupied the chief positions of power and tended to scorn the pretensions of the Creoles. And Spanish-born bureaucrats were naturally more responsive to the wishes of the king and often tried to ameliorate the condition of the Indians over the opposition of Creoles.

One opportunity the Creoles did gain under the Bourbons was to hold commissions in the local militias. Faced with war on the European continent, the expanding imperial ambitions of other nations, and limited financial and human resources in Europe, the Spanish government set out to expand and revitalize the colonial militias. Spanish officers were dispatched to train these part-time troops, and Creoles were then promoted to the rank of officers. The militia officers also gained for the first time the right to the military fuero. The officers thus combined upper-class background with the outward signs of authority; the troops themselves, of course, came from less privileged origins. In Brazil the locally wealthy and well connected also held commissions in the militia. In times of threatened attack, as often happened in the late eighteenth century, they were mobilized and got to display their authority and add to their prestige while learning the rudiments of military organization. But in eighteenth-century Brazil the regular army itself was largely officered by the Brazilian-born, and, among these, sons of the planter class were preferred in promotions. Only later were armies sent from Portugal.

Social conditions in Brazil differed from those in the highlands of Spanish America. The Indians living in Brazil at the time of first contact with Europeans had not been part of so-called "high civilizations" like the Aztecs or Incas but rather had roamed the wilds with bows and arrows in search of game, stopping in one place only long enough to plant and harvest some corn and manioc. For this reason, these Indians had not located sources of gold and precious stones, built large cities, or established kingdoms or empires. The Portuguese, despite diligent searching, were not to find these coveted supplies for two centuries. By that time the basic institutional structure of Brazil was set. Sugar had become the chief export crop and the principal activity of the settlers. The sugar plantation gave Brazil a rural cast; for instance, the isolated chapel with its plantation chaplain was the center of religious life rather than the city cathedral. Meanwhile, the Indian was rapidly eliminated from the coastal region and pushed back into the interior.

Instead of Indian laborers, African slaves worked the plantations in Brazil. Some 2.5 million enslaved blacks had been imported there by 1800. Despite the fact that in the eighteenth century the sugar economy was no longer growing, the slaves' work on the Brazilian plantations continued to be oriented by one principle: The master's profit was the end purpose of their labor. On the other hand, the long-standing practice of manumitting slaves to reward faithful service, to celebrate special occasions, or in exchange for cash (either already accumulated by the slave or promised in the future) had led to a large number of free blacks and mulattos. In Salvador there were even separate militia regiments for these free blacks and pardos, who prided themselves on their discipline and loyalty to established authority. But, if there seemed to be an easier acceptance of the free colored than in Spanish America, the Brazilian elites still saw the African Brazilians—be they free or slave—as a potential threat to the social order.

In both Brazil and Spanish America the colonial system engendered social tensions. In order for that system to work as envisioned, men had to be compelled to work to produce colonial products for colonial trade. Anyone who commanded others constantly felt the difficulty of getting them to do his will rather than theirs. At the same time, many in the colonial elite chafed at the restrictions placed upon them by the monopoly merchants, by authorities from the Iberian peninsula, and especially by tax collectors. In certain places they were all too eager to evade the rules and trade with the foreign interloper.

Some even thought that, better yet, they could oversee their own affairs entirely. But could they win that privilege without endangering their own control over the laboring many?

Religion and the Enlightenment

In solidifying the edifice of colonial rule, religion had provided a firm cement. Before the eighteenth century, state and Church in the Iberian world had been so closely related that they should be considered one; even a conceptual distinction between them may be misleading unless it is understood as merely a heuristic device. For centuries the Portuguese and Spanish kings had been granted patronage over the Church; that is, the Crown, in exchange for financing and fostering the preaching of the Gospel, received the right to make all appointments of churchmen. In addition, the Crown would collect the tithe, a tax for Church purposes. Even papal bulls could be published only after they had been approved by the king, who also controlled and limited the number of religious orders that sent members overseas and restricted the travels of individual friars. Finally, the Inquisition was primarily an arm of the state designed to maintain ideological purity.

It may have been fortunate that the state controlled the Church, for its enormous wealth, especially if one includes that of the religious orders, might otherwise have represented an unregulated and irresponsible power. The ordinary expenses of the bishops, cathedrals, and parish priests were paid by the state from the revenue derived from the tithe. In Portuguese America the state merged this revenue with its general fund and paid out fixed salaries, whereas in Spanish America the bishop was the king's agent in supervising the collection of the tithe and then dispensing the resulting funds. Consequently, in prosperous areas of Spanish America the bishop controlled extensive resources. Parish clergymen, besides their stipends, also received fees for baptisms, marriages, and the performance of other religious offices. In addition, both the secular Church and religious orders received numerous bequests, most often to pay for the saying of masses for the souls of the dead. These could represent a substantial portion of the deceased's estate. Once real property was given to such corporate bodies, it was rarely sold, either because it was inalienable by the terms of the bequest or because the Church, unlike individuals, was never forced to divide its property among its heirs. Furthermore, partly because of Church laws forbidding usury and partly because of its great wealth, the principal banker in Spanish America was the Church. As a result, it held foreclosable mortgages on a vast number of estates.

Much of this wealth was used to finance charitable institutions and mission work. Social services like hospitals and orphanages, which are today often thought of as at least partially the government's responsibility, were then carried on exclusively by lay organizations under the auspices of the Church, while regular orders typically ran schools and colleges. Although many of these institutions fell into disrepair and became merely sinecures for churchmen primarily interested in luxurious living in the cities, others continued to be vigorous centers of social concern. In addition, the imperial task of extending the frontiers of Iberian culture and power into the jungles of South and Central America and into the treeless plains and high deserts of North America was carried out by courageous missionaries.

The Church was not immune from change in the eighteenth century. The Bourbon kings maintained the ancient union of Church and state but were much more conscious of the Church as a separate entity. Probably for this reason, there was increasing friction between the Crown and the Church. The Church fuero was successively restricted, and it may be for this reason that many clergymen later joined revolutionary movements. The Bourbons also systematically reduced the power of the Inquisition. In the early nineteenth century they decreed that Church endowments should be exchanged for 3 percent public bonds, a step that not only alienated churchmen but created chaos in the credit system.

Religious orthodoxy had always been less important to the Portuguese, and the Spaniards looked upon them as degenerate worshipers of Baal. Both the Spanish and Portuguese expelled Jews from their countries, but the Portuguese were less adamant in their persecution. For the Spanish one precondition for migrating to Spanish America was the purity of one's "blood," that is, religion; but the Portuguese encouraged the "New Christian" converts from Judaism and their descendants to migrate to Brazil. Nevertheless, the Inquisition had also been active in Portugal, and Pombal now set to work to limit its power.

Since the Portuguese-Brazilian Church hierarchy was relatively weak and poor, Pombal did not feel compelled to attack it the way Charles III did, but Pombal was deeply suspicious of the Jesuits. He charged this religious order with plotting with the Spanish to prevent the extension of Portuguese boundaries in South America in areas where the Jesuits maintained missions. Like the Spanish Bourbons, Pombal resented the fact that this religious order was more loyal to the pope than to the king. Furthermore, the Jesuits in both Portuguese and Spanish America were among the most efficient administrators of property, owned some of the best land, competed successfully with the local merchants, operated the leading secondary schools, and, through their vigor and their drive, created intense jealousies wherever they went. Finally, in 1759 Pombal ordered their expulsion from all Portuguese territory. The Bourbons followed suit in 1767 for much the same reasons. Although the act was carried out simultaneously throughout the Spanish empire and preparations for it were kept as secret as could be done, it nevertheless resulted in uprisings among some Indians and other groups over whom the Jesuits had maintained a protective stance. Many colonists, however, welcomed the move.

All these measures, taken together, weakened the Church, one of the bulwarks of the Iberian empires. More: the conceptual distance between Church and state widened, so that these measures unwittingly undermined the belief that the state was God's surrogate on earth. As the ideological foundation of the old order suffered erosion, a new set of ideas gained a small but growing acceptance. These ideas were derived from the European intellectual movement that historians have dubbed "the Enlightenment."

During the eighteenth century the Enlightenment had a noticeable effect on colonial intellectuals and professionals. Not every aspect of this complex intellectual movement had an equal impact among them; they picked and chose from this smorgasbord of ideas according to their special needs. But it is no longer even necessary to attack the myth that Latin America was kept in cloistered isolation from all new ideas by a veritable iron curtain imposed by retrograde governments. The truth is that precisely these governments, led by "enlightened despots," injected a modern worldview into backward overseas domains, along with understandings of man and the world that the Enlightenment embodied. And the viceroys and judges themselves often organized literary societies, held soirées, and prided themselves on being as up to date in their ideas as they were in their French-inspired clothing styles. The upper and middle classes followed that example and saw themselves as part of European civilization, whether through meeting at coffeehouses, organizing balls, or talking about the most recent books arriving from overseas. On the other hand, the spread of the Enlightenment must not be exaggerated in societies within which only the narrowest fringe could even read and write.

Science, or rather a scientific epistemology or way of knowing—and all that it implies regarding human beings' place in the world—was the most important aspect of the new thought in Latin America. It implied a belief in reason and practicality. The avenues for communicating this new approach were not seriously restricted. Scientific expeditions working under official auspices were perhaps the most important. Several noted European astronomers, botanists, and geographers were sent out at royal expense to conduct studies, collect specimens, observe the stars, and make meticulous drawings. Some of the most conservative Spanish-American academic centers were, in the eighteenth century, gradually abandoning or manipulating the scholasticism inherited from medieval days and adopting the new approach to knowledge. Even at the relatively isolated University of Guatemala, for instance, the "new thought" was fully accepted by professors and dutifully repeated in student theses. In Brazil the viceroy founded a scientific society in 1772, and the Portuguese government funded a major ten-year scientific expedition to the Amazon beginning in 1783.

A striking example of the new scientific spirit in America was José Celestino Mutis (1732–1808), a Spanish physician who had moved to Bogotá in the early 1760s. As trained personnel were scarce, he was asked to teach mathematics and astronomy at the university, where he subsequently built an observatory and taught the Copernican system. With characteristic eighteenth-century curiosity, Mutis then began the study of botany and carried on an active correspondence with the Swedish scientist Carolus Linnaeus. The viceroy, with the encouragement of the Spanish government, provided Mutis with a subsidy to begin a vast botanical project to make a systematic collection of specimens and drawings of South American flora. His botanical work was carried on by his American-born pupil Francisco José de Caldas (1770–1816), who kept up an active correspondence and intellectual interchange with Benjamin Franklin, one of the most important Enlightenment thinkers in the New World. Eventually Caldas turned his attention to institutional obstacles to change.

The social and political ideas associated with the Enlightenment—

the social contract between rulers and ruled, the political and economic freedom of the individual, the importance of reason over revelation in guiding social policy, the belief in social progress through education—also invaded Latin America, although without the same official protection. In Spain the new ideas of Voltaire, Rousseau, and the French *philosophes* had been popularized by Benito Feijóo, and, although many of the original sources were banned by the Catholic *Index* of prohibited books, he and other writers spread their concepts far and near. Anyway, there were many well-educated Creoles who knew those works directly, and attempts to suppress the circulation of these views were always in vain (indeed, there was even a Spanish tradition dating from the sixteenth century that emphasized how rulers depended on the consent of the ruled). Libraries of famous and not-so-famous men in Brazil (for instance, those implicated in conspiracies uncovered in 1789 and 1798) included works by Voltaire, Montesquieu, and Condillac as well as the French *Encyclopédie*. Still, it was the scientific ideas that were more widespread, and it was only at the time of independence itself that the social and political implications of the new ideology became really important among Latin Americans.

Their understanding of these ideas by the early nineteenth century was deeply colored by the French Revolution. Many believed that it had been French thinkers who had wittingly or unwittingly encouraged the demands in France that the king summon the Estates Général in 1788 and it had been expectations raised by intellectuals that had fired the crowd that stormed the Bastille in 1789. So the response to Enlightenment ideas now varied according to whether one saw these events favorably or not. The class basis of the French movement was clearly understood only by more conservative Latin Americans, and they abhorred the result. The radical or reform-minded ones, despite their own aristocratic or semiaristocratic origins, greatly admired the Declaration of the Rights of Man enacted by the French Assembly that guaranteed both the legal freedom of the individual and private property rights against government interference. Only a few radicals, however, failed to condemn the violence and bloodshed of the subsequent Reign of Terror directed by the French National Convention, the Committee of Public Safety, and Robespierre. Most sighed in relief at the conservative reaction that culminated in the seizure of power by Napoleon Bonaparte in 1799. As he led French armies that then swept across Europe, many Latin Americans admired him for his daring and his personal verve, even if a few were troubled by the decline of individual freedom under his rule. But freedom was now associated with the Terror, and the ideology of liberty was seen as a two-edged sword to be drawn only at great risk. These conclusions were further bolstered by the record in Haiti.

Haiti

Two colonies in the Americas became independent before the Spanish and Portuguese ones, and their experiences had a marked impact upon the movements examined here. The first was that of the United States. The course of its war for independence is too well known to be recited here, but one point did not escape the Latin American elites: slave owners such as Washington and Jefferson were able to win their country's independence without ending slavery. Indeed, it has been argued by Edmund S. Morgan that in the United States the slavery of blacks made possible the ideal of freedom for the whites.[5] In any case, those leaders in Latin America who desired freedom from colonial rule for their countries without personal freedom for their workers were encouraged by the North American example. The opposite effect resulted from the example of Haiti.

Haiti, or Saint-Domingue, as it was then known, was a prosperous French colony in the Caribbean producing coffee, indigo, cotton, and especially sugar on the western end of the island of Española (Hispaniola). The shape of the country is that of a crescent with two peninsulas pointing to the west at the northern and southern edge of a huge bay. It had been a haven for buccaneers in the seventeenth century and was formally annexed by France in 1697. By 1780 its ports teemed with French ships, and French monopoly merchants profited handsomely from its trade. The plantations were worked by a half-million slaves, while only 30,000 whites and some 28,000 free mulattos made up the rest of the population. The richest plantations lay along the northern peninsula, so it was there that the largest number of slaves was concentrated.

---

[5] Edmund S. Morgan, *American Slavery, American Freedom* (New York: Norton, 1975).

Society was sharply divided into distinct groups. By the 1780s the wealthy planters, like many of those in Spanish and Portuguese America, were becoming dissatisfied with their lack of political power and mercantilist trade restrictions. In the subsequent course of events they hoped for local rule within the old French monarchy and were generally unsympathetic toward the French Revolution. Poorer whites—artisans, tradesmen, and the descendants of the original indentured servants—favored the Revolution and the end of the monarchy. A third group, made up of free mulattos, were ambitious and hardworking. Several became planters, and many acquired smaller tracts of land in the less fertile and hillier southern peninsula or along the north-south axis linking the two peninsulas. By 1789 they owned approximately a third of the colony's land and a quarter of the slaves. Naturally they resented the racial discrimination that they suffered at the hands of the whites, be they rich planters or, even worse, poor whites, but they did not wish the end of slavery. After midcentury a series of legal restrictions had been placed upon them, forbidding them to bear arms or wear certain kinds of clothes and making the penalties for violation of any law more severe for them than for whites. The French Declaration of the Rights of Man seemed to promise them equality at last. Finally, there were the slaves themselves. Probably two-thirds of them had been born in Africa, as the slave trade was intense and mortality rates high. They were treated harshly, perhaps more so than anywhere else in the Americas. In addition to these four groups, of course, there were the Frenchmen who filled government positions and were charged with maintaining the commercial monopoly on behalf of the merchants in France. Ironically, these merchants formed one of the groups in France that most enthusiastically backed the French Revolution but were not likely to support any alteration of the status quo in the colony.

When King Louis XVI of France was finally compelled to summon a meeting of the Estates Général in 1788, the planters of Saint-Domingue determined to send delegates and try to secure self-rule. Only six of the thirty-seven delegates were actually seated and that only after lengthy debate; but those six articulately called for the loosening of the trade monopoly and the appointment of a fellow planter as administrator in the colony. Unstated, but even more important to them, was their intention that there be no alteration in the colonial social order. In this last point they were opposed by the emancipationist French Société des Amis de Noirs and by lobbyists financed by the rich mulatto planters of Saint-Domingue.

The far-reaching social transformations the Revolution wrought in France could not fail to have repercussions in the colony. When news reached the town of Le Cap of the storming of the Bastille in 1789, the poorer whites rioted and demanded the dismissal of the royally appointed governor. The rich planters responded by creating their own colonial assembly (later replaced by one officially sanctioned by the French Assembly) from which both mulattos and poor whites were excluded. This assembly passed a number of regulations that, taken together, amounted to a virtual declaration of independence, although its members insisted on their continued loyalty to the king. They refused to take orders from the French Assembly, so the French governor and garrison, taking these actions as a challenge, finally forced the entire assembly to flee the island. Meanwhile, the mulattos, angered by their exclusion from the deliberations, rose up in protest; but they were quickly defeated, their leaders imprisoned and cruelly tortured. From Paris contradictory instructions arrived, contributing to the general unrest.

Such signs of disarray among the free may have been the spark that set off the slave revolt in August 1791 in the plantation region of the northern peninsula. Although it has been argued that French officials actually instigated it to bring the whites and mulattos to heel, surely no great impetus was needed to encourage the slaves, who were well informed of events and often had a clear sense of their goals and opportunities, to take this moment to rebel. Their pent-up rage found expression in the destruction of some two hundred sugar mills and six hundred coffee estates during just the first eight days of their movement. Soon they were in control of the entire northern region outside the towns, but fighting continued for months with cruelty practiced by both sides upon those they captured.

Later the same year (1791) mulattos again rose up in the other parts of the colony and this time, with white planters dispossessed in the north, they met with considerable success. They declared that their government would be open to all who possessed a given income except white planters; by these restrictions they excluded both the poor whites and ex-slaves, leaving wealthy mulattos in sole control of the center and south.

The French Assembly attempted to regain authority over the rebel-

Slave Revolt in Saint-Domingue (Haiti)

lious colony by dispatching army after army. But at this point European political-diplomatic events impinged directly on those in Saint-Domingue. At the end of 1791 an alliance of several countries had been formed in Europe to oppose the French Revolution and reimpose absolute monarchy in France. Spain joined the effort and instructed its officials in the Spanish part of the island of Española to attack the French. Ironically, to back their anti-Revolutionary effort in Europe, the Spanish offered to support the ex-slaves in their continuing struggle for freedom in Saint-Domingue. The British also joined the anit-Revolutionary alliance in Europe, also decided to attack the French colony, but did not side with the slaves. Instead, they supported the planters who, after all, had declared their loyalty to the French king. In August 1793 the French governor, in an attempt to regain the upper hand militarily against the British, declared the freedom of all slaves (a measure that was ratified by the French National Convention in February 1794 by a decree of emancipation). The governor's stratagem gradually had its desired effect, and in 1794 ex-slaves began to abandon the Spanish and side with the French, gradually driving out the British. With their defeat in 1797, most of the white planters, whom the British had backed, fled the island.

At the head of the blacks was Pierre-Domingue Toussaint l'Ouverture. Born as a slave, he had become a trusted coachman, learned to read, and acquired an education on his own. He had joined the slave rebellion soon after its outbreak and gradually became its leader. It was he who had engineered an alliance between the ex-slaves and the Spanish, and he was among the first to agree to join forces with the French against the British after news of the decree of emancipation had arrived. For he considered himself a Frenchman, trusted in the definitive abolition of slavery by the National Convention, and backed the principles of the French Revolution. The French made him a general, and he gradually took over the direction of the military effort, making even the French-born officers into his virtual subordinates. Once the British were gone, and aided by the African-born General Jean-Jacques Dessalines, he set to work against the mulatto faction. It was an ugly war, and some 10,000 mulattos were killed.

From 1797 to 1801 Toussaint's rule went unquestioned. He promulgated a constitution that maintained a nominal tie to France but granted the French government practically no authority regarding internal affairs. The ports of the "colony" were opened to the trade of any nation. Although Toussaint insisted on identifying himself with the French, Saint-Domingue was to all intents and purposes now a free country. Increasingly, it was called Haiti, the name for the area used by the pre-Columbian natives. Securing for himself from the newly elected assembly the post of governor-general for life, Toussaint set about restoring law and order as well as economic prosperity. He fostered the renewed planting of sugar, rebuilt the irrigation system, and forced ex-slaves to work the plantations, now with the title of "cultivators." Sugar production soared, and Toussaint was widely popular even among the workers he compelled, although his authoritarianism was resented by his immediate subordinates.

Napoleon Bonaparte, however, had other plans for the island. Napoleon dreamed of building a French colonial empire that would stretch from Louisiana to the Amazon. Haiti was crucial to his plans. He had only contempt for a black man who claimed to be French. As soon as he had secured peace with the British at Amiens in 1801, he dispatched an army of twenty-five thousand troops commanded by his brother-in-law General Charles Victor Emmanuel Leclerc, instructing him to reestablish French authority and restore the social order as it had once been. Toussaint resisted this army as best he could, but he was unable to convince all his followers that Leclerc was an enemy (for Leclerc's instructions were secret). Toussaint suffered several defeats, was forced to surrender in 1802, and was sent in chains to France, where he died in prison the following year.

Once news arrived in Haiti that the French were reenslaving the blacks in other French colonies, however, a new rebellion broke out, this time led by Dessalines and Henri Christophe. They understood that either Haiti must be independent or blacks would lose their freedom. While they were still gathering their forces, a yellow fever epidemic struck the French army. Within weeks eight thousand men died, including Leclerc himself, and fresh reinforcements from France suffered the same fate. Then war began again in Europe, and Napoleon had to scrap his dreams of an American empire. He sold Louisiana to the United States and recalled what troops still survived in the Caribbean island. On January 1, 1804, Dessalines proclaimed the independence of Haiti.

The subsequent fate of the ex-French colony was not a happy one. Dessalines declared himself an emperor and ruled absolutely. He and his followers discriminated sharply against the remaining poor whites and the mulattos. In 1806 he was assassinated, and the resulting power vacuum resulted in civil war and anarchy. At one point the country broke into two, a black republic in the northern peninsula and a mulatto one in the rest of the country. In the end the mulattos emerged as dominant throughout, but never with absolute authority and legitimacy. And the years of war had left a devastated country. The ex-slaves preferred to raise their food on small plots they themselves controlled rather than toil on plantations to produce an export crop while they went hungry.

Haiti's example struck fear into the hearts of the planter class in Spanish and Portuguese America. Like those in Saint-Domingue, they desired free trade and political autonomy. But they saw themselves surrounded not only by mestizos or mulattos who desired social recognition, but by slaves or oppressed Indians, whose rage could easily be unleashed by any sign of division among the white ruling groups and most of all by any disruptive war. They understood that what had begun in Haiti as an effort by the elites to secure independence had ended in the destruction of those very elites. Francisco de Miranda, one of the precursors of and early participants in the Latin American independence movement, said, "much as I desire the independence and liberty of the New World, I fear anarchy and revolution even more. God forbid that other countries suffer the same fate as Saint-Domingue. . . . Better they should remain another century under the barbarous and senseless oppression of Spain."[6] Similarly in Brazil, a man who in 1791 had spoken out in favor of the "equality of men," the very next year confessed his fear that what had happened in Haiti would also occur in Brazil, "which God forbidding I shall never see."[7] And he was right to fear such developments: in 1805 "black and half-breed" members of the militia were found wearing on their chests "portraits of Dessalines, Emperor of the Blacks in S. Domingue."[8]

* * *

The eighteenth century had surely been a century of change for Latin America. The increasing demand in northern Europe for colonial products was matched by the export of a new, capitalistic ideology, whether expressed in laissez-faire economic theory or a vision of the social contract in politics, whether attacking mercantilism or absolutism. The exclusive right of metropolitan merchants to control all trade to the colonies seemed less and less acceptable to those who produced cattle hides or sugar or cacao. The increasingly self-conscious Creole elites, pleased with their newly acquired military ranks in the militia, desired a still larger decision-making role. But the experience of Haiti made these elites sharply aware of the potential dangers for them of pushing too far, too fast toward local autonomy in societies built upon the labor of unwilling workers. They knew it would be upon these workers that they would have to rely as soldiers if armed conflict were to result. Nevertheless, it was now possible to

---

[6] Quoted in Anthony Pagden, *Spanish Imperialism and the Political Imagination* (New Haven: Yale University Press, 1990), p. 12.

[7] Quoted in Kenneth R. Maxwell, "The Generation of the 1790s and the Idea of Luso-Brazilian Empire," in Dauril Alden, ed., *Colonial Roots of Modern Brazil, Papers of the Newberry Library Conference* (Berkeley: University of California Press, 1973), p. 117.

[8] Luiz Mott, "A escravatura . . . ," *Revista do Instituto de Estudos Brasileiros*, no. 14 (1973), 132n.

think of such action because the ideological underpinnings of the two Iberian empires had been frayed both by the emerging state-church conflict and by the Enlightenment. Perhaps even more important were the legal theories that informed common understandings regarding the tie between subject and king, theories that were rooted in the works of sixteenth-century thinkers and the experiences of three hundred years.

The divisions of Latin American societies implied different visions of the future. Whereas for some "freedom" meant the end of forced labor, for others it meant an end of the colonial mercantile monopoly and for still others it signified individual liberty whether political or economic. As the nineteenth century opened, no one expected the complete rupture of the Portuguese and Spanish empires, but many sensed that the old certainties had collapsed. While some viewed the prospect with enthusiasm, others saw it with alarm.

Chapter Two
Reactions to Change

E ach area of Latin America reacted in its own way to eighteenth-century change. The lure of closer trade with northern Europe and the usefulness of Enlightenment ideas depended on the configuration of elite interests. Social tensions varied from place to place as well. The subsequent courses of the respective independence movements in the nineteenth century, therefore, were to vary too. This chapter examines the bases of these differences before independence and projects their effects into the ensuing struggles. In Argentina, Chile, and Uruguay we see the contrasting weight of mercantile exclusivism and note how, by the end of the colonial period, a desire for regional autonomy sometimes outweighed any pressure toward independence from Spain. In Venezuela, Mexico, Peru, and Brazil we see how social conflict or its all-too-visible possibility shaped elite attitudes toward Spanish rule. The desire to modify the social structure and open it up to individual mobility varied greatly from place to place.

Argentina

REGIONS   The Viceroyalty of Río de la Plata lacked geographical and historical unity and was unwieldly as a government unit from the

37

time of its establishment in 1776. It contained a variety of regions: the massive Andean ranges then referred to as Alto Peru and since renamed Bolivia; the piedmont regions that are now in Argentina, which included the wine-producing zone around Mendoza, the sugar-rich areas around Tucumán, and the proud and ancient university city of Córdoba; and the steaming lowlands that are today Paraguay. At the center of the viceroyalty lay the vast pampas, or grassy plains, that stretched for nearly five hundred miles west of the city of Buenos Aires. Cattle roamed free and wild on the pampas, multiplying rapidly during two hundred years of neglect. Almost as wild as the cattle were the gauchos, or plainsmen, who slaughtered the cattle for their hides, although nearer the city of Buenos Aires wheat farming predominated. And, finally, the viceroyalty included the rolling grasslands that today are Uruguay.

The defense of this last region against incursions from the Portuguese was the chief reason for the introduction of viceregal pomp and ceremony into the otherwise bedraggled country village of Buenos Aires. The Portuguese had established a settlement directly across the estuary of the Río de la Plata in 1680, and from this base they had carried on successful smuggling activity to the mining regions in the Andes. Whenever war broke out in eighteenth-century Europe, Spain and Portugal were on opposite sides of the struggle, and repercussions were immediate in this region. During the fighting the Spaniards usually drove the Portuguese out of the eastern bank of the estuary and pushed them into what is today southern Brazil, but at the ensuing peace conference the Portuguese would regain much of the lost territory and then surreptitiously extend their control still farther into this sparsely settled region. Finally, in 1776 King Charles III dispatched to the region ten thousand troops and a viceroy charged with putting a stop to Portuguese expansion. Although the king was momentarily successful in this goal, the region remained a pawn fought over by Portuguese- and Spanish-speaking peoples even after the viceroyalty was succeeded by independent republics.

A great rivalry existed between the two cities in the region: Buenos Aires and Montevideo. The harbor was better at Montevideo than at Buenos Aires, the surrounding region was far richer in pastoral resources than the pampas around Buenos Aires, and the first plant for preparing jerked beef had been erected there. Yet the Bourbons favored Buenos Aires. The appointment of a viceroy to Buenos Aires exacerbated these tensions, and deep and ingrained hostility between the two cities was the final result.

The Decree of Free Trade of 1778 had even more far-reaching results. Buenos Aires was permitted to trade directly with Spain instead of indirectly via Lima and the circuitous route that led along the Pacific coast through Panamá and across the Caribbean and Atlantic to Spain. The transformations were profound. No longer strangled by isolation from international markets and foreign sources of supply, no longer forced to survive only by virtue of its smugglers' ability, the region around Buenos Aires experienced rapid economic growth. Prices of imports declined, and a large legal export business developed, although principally through the hands of Spanish-born monopoly merchants. The silver from the fabled mine at Potosí, which had earlier gone through Lima, now flowed through Buenos Aires, and wealth accumulated in the hands of those merchants. In addition, pastoral products were increasingly important exports by the early nineteenth century: hides, horns, jerked beef, and tallow, derived from the wild cattle that roamed the pampas. Buenos Aires, whose inhabitants were called *porteños*, became the port for a vast and wealthy area, exporting not only to Spain, but also to the Caribbean. The population of the city grew from twelve thousand in 1750 to forty thousand by 1800.

Satisfaction with the trade reform was short-lived. By the end of the century, most of the cattle had been slaughtered, and the years of unrestrained prosperity had only served to whet the appetite for a still easier exchange of products between Buenos Aires and other European nations, particularly England. Furthermore, Spain lagged behind England in her ability to supply manufactured goods and continued to burden all exchange with onerous taxes designed to bolster her own faltering finances. Spain merely stood in the way of continued economic expansion by preventing a better balance in the prices of exports and imports.

Yet Spain would not open the port of Buenos Aires to the trade of European nations because this would have destroyed her monopoly merchants, whose political power was considerable, and might have alienated the traditionally loyal western cities, particularly Lima. So, by the beginning of the nineteenth century, greater prosperity for the pampas became logically synonymous with independence from Spain, even when that conclusion was not actually expressed.

GROUPS   By 1810 there was a complete lack of consensus among the divergent elite groups as to the organization of society and its government. Subsequently the divisions became ever more intense, and new sources of friction were added to old ones. Four issues served as principal sources of disagreement. First in ultimate importance was the issue of social structure: Should the old corporate society, hierarchic in conception and religious in basis, be continued, or should it be replaced by a society of free individuals, vertically mobile regardless of original "condition"? Second, and most immediately in evidence before 1810, was the issue of trade: Should it be monopolized by Spain or opened to other nations? Third, and most apparent after 1810, was the issue of type of government: Should Argentina be ruled by a king—any king—or be a republic? And finally there remained what would become the most enduring issue: the division deriving from divergent regional interests between "federalists," who demanded provincial and local autonomy, and their opponents, who dreamt of a unified, centralized government. Although the issues are simply defined, they were not simply resolved, for individuals grouped and regrouped around each question without consistency. Even similar economic interests, social relationships, or educational levels did not ensure a common position on many of these issues.

Creole intellectuals were the most visible early group to express opinions. By "intellectuals" I mean, here and in the remainder of this book, to include many doctors, lawyers, and priests, as well as professors, teachers, journalists, and other writers. Chiefly concentrated in Buenos Aires but also existing in minute numbers in the interior cities, on the whole these men came from the upper middle class. They adopted the ideals of the Enlightenment, the French and American revolutions, and the desire to transform their country accordingly. Such men as Mariano Moreno (1778–1811), Manuel Belgrano (1770–1820), and Bernardino Rivadavia (1780–1845) were typical. These intellectuals believed that the natural laws that ruled over economic and social affairs required the end of commercial restrictions, freedom of speech and press, and the attraction of immigrants from the non-Spanish world. The ideas of Adam Smith, Jean-Jacques Rousseau, and later Jeremy Bentham greatly attracted them. They divided, however, on the ideal form of government. Some wanted a monarchy on the British model; others, a republic. Some wanted a strong, centralized government that could impose change

upon the backward interior; others, more doctrinaire, felt that freedom could be preserved only through local self-government and a
loose federation of sovereign states. When independence became a
reality, these divisions loomed even larger.

Buenos Aires was, more than any other viceregal capital, a particularly commercial city, an entrepôt above all else. Merchants held a
prominent place in its affairs, while Creole landowners, who had just
begun to carve estates out of the open range, remained quite dependent on them. The merchants can be divided into two groups: the
Spanish-born agents or intermediaries of monopoly merchants, who
preferred to maintain the old regime and who dominated the newly
created merchant guild; and the moderately wealthy Creole merchants, who envied the formers' position. The latter shared the
intellectuals' belief in the necessity for direct trade with northern
Europe but were not as committed to the general transformation of
the social structure as the intellectuals were. The more conservative
merchants believed that monarchy was the best form of government.
All the Buenos Aires merchants, however, wanted a centralized government, for they believed that this type of government would help
place economic power into their hands and prevent internal tariff
barriers from weakening their control over the country at large. After
1810, when the old trading system ceased to exist, the merchants
became more united.

The merchants in the interior cities differed sharply from their
counterparts in Buenos Aires. They looked back nostalgically to the
days of their own importance, when trade had been oriented toward
Lima. So they opposed the rupture of the old trading system and the
centralization of government in Buenos Aires. The craftsmen and
agrarian interests of the interior naturally took the same stand.

The cattle ranchers in the huge province of Buenos Aires were
anxious to establish direct commercial connections with the consuming centers of northern Europe and were willing to go along with the
suggestions of the intellectuals that the social structure must be
transformed. They were upwardly mobile, lusting after wealth, and
they had little use for the ancient modalities of social hierarchy, for
the practices of entail and primogeniture, or for privilege and monopoly. After 1810 they gradually became more preoccupied with gaining
power and protecting their interests. Not ideologically committed to
central government, they managed outwardly to support federalists

in the subsequent internecine fighting while instituting de facto strong centralized government whenever they occupied the seat of power. Ranchers in Uruguay, on the other hand, clearly demanded local autonomy.

Other groups were less significant in determining the course of events surrounding the struggle for independence. Poorer whites throughout the region, anxious to preserve their social superiority but threatened with downward mobility because of economic changes they did not fully understand, developed a strong antipathy toward those born in Spain. Meanwhile, the mixed-race gauchos, who had once roamed unfettered across the grasslands, began to find themselves reduced to hired hands on private lands belonging to others. This process had not gone far enough, however, to provoke organized or widespread social discontent, and the elites could safely ignore gaucho interests for the nonce and, in fact, mobilize them into rival armies with the promise of personal gain. These cowboys proved to be excellent soldiers in the civil wars that accompanied independence.

There were, in short, many distinct groups and different regions in Argentina, and it is not surprising that their reactions to the independence movement were not characterized by uniformity.

Chile

REGIONS   Just as the creation of the Viceroyalty of Río de la Plata reduced the area under the jurisdiction of the viceroy in Lima, so too did the formation in 1778 of the Captaincy-General of Chile. Although this area along the southwest coast of South America nominally formed part of the Viceroyalty of Peru, the effective king's agent was the captain-general, who ruled from Santiago itself.

The Captaincy-General of Chile contained only one important region: the central valley, running for six hundred miles north and south between the towering Andes on the east and the lower coastal range on the west. The land was chiefly used for the cultivation of wheat and other cereals, some viniculture, and the production of fruits, which were dried and exported. Cattle hides, pack mules, and small amounts of copper were also exported. All these goods went primarily to supply the market at Lima or the mines of Bolivia except the copper, which mostly went to Spain. The chief city in Chile was Santiago, but Concepción at the southern extreme of the central valley proved increasingly important.

GROUPS   The central valley had been won from the fierce Araucanian Indians two and a half centuries before, but in the heavily forested area south of the valley some one hundred thousand still remained unconquered. Those who had been conquered had been absorbed through racial mixture, and mestizos formed the bulk of the Chilean population. They were tenant farmers, farmhands, menial workers, domestic servants, and skilled artisans. The agricultural workers were held in a virtual bondage to their landlords, the hacendados, but still considered themselves privileged in comparison with others who wandered from place to place in search of some land to plant in exchange for service. They did not pose an overt threat to the social order.

Some Creole landowners claimed descent from the original conquistadors and hid their small admixture of Indian blood. But in the eighteenth century this class was renovated by intermarriage with the sons and daughters of Basque immigrants, whose industry in commerce rapidly enabled them to accumulate considerable wealth. Old and new landowners cherished the right to entail their properties, purchase titles of nobility, and live in relative splendor in the cities with only occasional visits to their estates, sometimes to command the militia which they officered. They were frequently the victims of exploitation by Peruvian merchants, however, who manipulated the price of wheat, and Chileans felt the dunning pressures placed on them by the Peruvian counting houses that financed their opulent lifestyle. Furthermore, Peruvians also controlled the carrying trade at the Chilean port of Valparaiso; by refusing to supply shipping at certain moments, they forced down the price of the exportable grain of Chile. The landowners, therefore, welcomed the Bourbons' trade reform, which allowed them to sell their grain all along the Pacific coast and to expand their exports to Argentina. The construction of a road for wheeled vehicles from the central valley to the port city of Valparaiso had stimulated the economy, as had the opening of a route across the Andes to the Argentine city of Mendoza, with links to

Buenos Aires. They did not seriously contemplate the possibility of exporting their goods to Europe and so did not demand a still freer trade.

The merchants of Santiago and its port, Valparaiso, were mostly Spanish-born subagents of Lima houses or agents of Spanish firms. Some Creoles were also merchants; they participated actively in contraband trade, but the influx of goods legally imported from Europe had by the 1800s already saturated the meager Chilean market and exhausted all available currency. Many merchants in legitimate and illegal trade went bankrupt. Moreover, the long struggle between merchants in Santiago and those in Lima culminated in the success of the former: they were granted the right to establish their own merchant guild, and a mint was established in Santiago. Along with the Bourbon system of so-called free trade, these measures helped to quell most of their complaints.

In Santiago, Valparaiso, and Concepción, a small group of intellectuals was active in the last years of the eighteenth century. Swept on especially by the reforms being carried out in Spain and the ideas being propagated there but also by the ideas of Adam Smith and the French philosophes, these men were able to move in at crucial moments to influence the course of events. Since they could not make a particularly strong case for the right to export products directly to Europe, they found other issues: They played upon the dissatisfaction of both the merchants and landowners over taxes imposed by Spain, especially those collected at the end of the century to fight the English and sometimes the French, and the age-long resentment over the lack of political power. The intellectuals maintained that prosperity would come only when Chile was controlled by Chileans, by which, of course, they meant the small crust of Creole aristocracy. The diversification of agriculture, the establishment of industries, and the introduction of modern techniques were all dependent, they said, upon a philosophy of government that had, as its chief aim, development rather than the immediate supply of revenues to the mother country. Once the revenues remained in Chile, progressive measures could be taken to facilitate rather than hinder the economy, and Chileans could take a stronger stand vis-à-vis the Peruvian merchants. Playing upon these ideas, the intellectuals managed to widen the circle of their listeners, but they would never have been able to do much if it were not for the constitutional crisis that overtook the Spanish empire at the time.

Comparisons

Chile, like Argentina, would move relatively early toward measures tending to break the imperial lines of authority. The intellectuals of both regions offered a rationale for this action, although they chose to emphasize different issues; and the desire to make decisions for themselves characterized both elites. In both Chile's central valley and the region around Buenos Aires, the landowners felt no threat from the changing patterns of trade, unlike the landowners of western Argentina, who faced ruin. But, as heirs to ancient families, the landowners of Chile held more conservative views than did the arriviste cattle ranchers of eastern Argentina.

One is struck by three other differences. First, the possibility of direct exports of local products to northern Europe was of overriding importance in Argentina but hardly considered in Chile. Second, the promise of cheaper imports was much more attractive to Argentina than to Chile. Third, Chile was more concerned with the preeminence of Lima, which was weakening under the Bourbons, than with throwing off the yoke of Spanish power; as was true for Uruguayans, the rivalry between colonial centers often loomed larger than the conflict between Creoles and Spaniards. Finally—and as a logical consequence—the hostility toward monopoly merchants was higher in Buenos Aires than in Santiago. Thus the origins of the Latin American independence movements can already be seen to vary from country to country. This is even clearer as we move to Venezuela and Mexico, where the relationship of lords and servants eventually loomed paramount.

Venezuela

REGIONS   The Viceroyalty of New Granada included at its eastern portion the area that is today Venezuela. Venezuela had been named a Captaincy-General in 1777 and thus was practically removed from the jurisdiction of the viceroy in Bogotá.

Along its northern coast the hot, humid climate was ideal for the production of tobacco, indigo, and especially cacao. In the higher elevations of the piedmont immediately to the south of the coast coffee bushes grew. Large plantations oriented toward profit making were important to the economy during the eighteenth century, and they were principally worked by African slaves supplied by English and other traders. The owners lived in cities in the mountain range running parallel to the coast from east to west, or in the Andean spur reaching deep into the region from the southwest. South of the coastal range and east of the Andes are the treeless plains, or *llanos*, swampy in the rainy season, scorched in the dry, beyond which runs the muddy water of the Orinoco River. To the south of it lay the forbidding jungle that stretched to the Amazon River.

GROUPS   Pushed by their desire to ship ever-larger quantities of plantation products, landowners bought ever-greater numbers of black slaves. By 1800 there were some eighty-seven thousand slaves, not counting the thousands who had run away. It did not take much perspicacity for slaveowners to feel the simmering discontent of their workers. Alexander von Humboldt, the German scientist who visited Venezuela in 1799, noted that this reality braked any enthusiasm for independence, for slaveowners "believed that in revolutions they would run the risk of losing their slaves."[1] Their fears became even greater after some three hundred slaves revolted in 1795, sacking plantations, killing the planters, and proclaiming their desire to follow the Haitian example and adopt "the law of the French, the republic, the freedom of slaves."[2] Four years later another unsuccessful re-volt—this one of free pardos in the militia—actually received help from Haiti. The slaves and the pardos together outnumbered the whites two to one. Pardos rubbed shoulders with new immigrants from Spain and the Canaries as tradesmen and artisans and intermar-ried with them.

Many free pardos sought to escape the master-and-man relation-ship characteristic of the plantations and the discriminatory treatment they encountered in the cities by fleeing to the llanos. Mixing with the Indians and mestizos of this region, the pardos joined them in cattle raising. Taking their name from the llanos, the *llaneros*, or cowboys,

---

[1] Quoted in John Lynch, *The Spanish-American Revolutions, 1808–1826* (New York: Norton, 1973), p. 190.

[2] Quoted in ibid., p. 193.

roamed free and careless, living to drink, gamble, and kill, always fiercely loyal to those demigods who commanded their loyalty as much because of their machismo and charisma as because of their prowess with the lasso and machete. The llaneros despised the way of life of the sedentary Creole planters and deeply distrusted their ambitions.

The Creole landowners were often at odds with the merchants despite their common social elitism. The merchants who were most disliked were the commercial representatives of the Caracas Company, a monopoly enterprise organized under royal auspices in 1728. Its creation had been prompted by the mushrooming growth of contraband trade. Modeled on the East and West India companies of the English and the Dutch and opened to the investment and direction of enterprising Basques, the company policed the coast and drove away the smugglers, stimulated cacao production, introduced new crops to diversify production, and returned profits reaching 20 percent a year. But the landowners were less than satisfied with the Caracas Company for it manipulated prices. When the company finally dissolved in the 1780s, it left behind a heritage of rancor against Spanish merchants.

Society in the cities was rigidly stratified. The landowning aristocracy—few in number but rich in fortune—carefully maintained their distance from "inferiors." Insisting upon the purity of their own racial heritage, they were alarmed at any "uppity" behavior by pardos. Racial feeling became particularly intense toward the end of the eighteenth century because an increasing number of pardos with industry and drive had achieved moderate wealth. Sometimes they even became the landowners' creditors, causing further alienation. Racial tensions were further exacerbated by the newly arrived Spaniards, who thought such attitudes ridiculous and proffered business opportunities and government posts to the pardos.

Grievances were often vented in the cabildos, which enjoyed more prestige and exercised more power than other cabildos in Spanish America because the Spanish government neglected the area. This neglect encouraged the members of the cabildos to think that they were the arbiters of their own affairs. The existence of several cities of more or less equal wealth and the absence of a viceroy, leaving only a captain-general to rule in Caracas, probably contributed to their sense of independence.

When the Bourbons ended this era of "salutary neglect" and began to tighten the reins of command toward the end of the century, their actions were resented. Then the European wars at the turn of the century were a further irritation, for taxes were increased; French and English ships, according to Spain's shifting alliances, alternately raided the port towns; and workers had to leave the plantations to defend the coast. On the eve of independence Venezuela seethed with discontent.

Mexico

REGIONS   The Viceroyalty of New Spain, stretching from Oregon to Central America, was the shining star in the Spanish imperial firmament. New Spain had a population of 6.5 million, more than any other viceroyalty, and it was also the most prosperous one. Principally because of its silver mines, the viceroyalty supplied two-thirds of all the revenues Spain derived from its empire, in addition to subsidizing imperial administrations in other colonies.

At the center of the country, both topographically and politically, lay Mexico City, embedded in a delightful valley at an altitude of almost eight thousand feet. In 1800 it held about 140,000 people, making it one of the largest cities in the world. Northward from this valley stretch two ranges in a somewhat lopsided V. The western range merges with the Rocky Mountains; the eastern range is shorter and ends around Monterrey. Northwest of Mexico City is the city of Guanajuato, the center of one of the most prosperous areas in Mexico. Fabulously productive silver mines lay in the hills about the city, and a rich agricultural and pastoral region supplied it and the mines with food and woolens. West of it, the burgeoning administrative and commercial center of Guadalajara was also the center of an agriculturally prosperous region. Further north, in more arid sections, cattle raising predominated, and more rich mines were located at San Luis Potosí and Zacatecas. East of Mexico City, in another fertile valley, lay the city of Puebla, a textile center. Toward the south the knotty mountains dissolve into strands that separate tropical valleys from cool highland ones. In one of the latter lay the city of Oaxaca, the center of a large, self-sufficient region of Indian villages that also produced indigo dye. Along the Balsas River, draining into the Pacific, and in the hot, humid plains that stretch to the Gulf of Mexico sugar, cacao, and tobacco plantations added to Mexico's export wealth and helped diversify its economy. Imports flowed in legally from Spain through Veracruz and illegally from other countries through every cove and sleepy harbor on the Caribbean coast. These goods then competed with those produced by craftsmen in highland cities, such as Puebla. On the Pacific coast Acapulco was the terminal point of a prosperous trade with the Philippines, to which Mexicans shipped silver in exchange for silks and other Oriental products. Transport between and among these different regions was almost entirely by mule train.

GROUPS   Mexico's increasing prosperity produced marked social tensions, for some groups and individuals were on the rise, while others were in decline. At the top of the social pyramid, as elsewhere in Spanish America, were Spaniards. Mexico's wealth attracted a large number of them to administer the bureaucracy that channeled revenues to Spain and to represent the interests of monopoly merchants. The Bourbon reforms had lessened the Creole hopes of participating in this uppermost strata, although they simultaneously unsettled the trading patterns that had once so exclusively benefited the Spanish merchants.

Immediately below this administrative and commercial elite were two other groups. One may be characterized as consisting of *nouveaux riches*. They had recently accumulated staggering fortunes: They had invested mercantile capital—their own or borrowed—in plantations and especially in mines, some of which proved to be bonanzas. Frequently either Spanish immigrants or the sons of immigrants, they had succeeded through great energy, ambition, good contacts, and luck. They sometimes blamed Spain for any obstacles they encountered in their attempt to rise even further or faster, but their loyalties were divided: Whereas their economic interests tied them to Mexico, their social roots made them sympathetic to Spain.

Another group, often in decline, were the Creole descendants of the conquistadors or at least of old-time settlers. These Creoles had rested too long on the glories of their antecedents and had paid too little attention to cultivating their inheritance. Nevertheless, they desperately clung to the vestiges of their former position, and one of these was often a proprietary seat on a cabildo. They inclined to the professions, especially law, for through its practice, without dirtying their hands, they could maintain appearances. They also entered the clergy or became teachers. They resented the lack of more positions for themselves in government, the Church, and overseas commerce. They often provided the intellectual justification for rebellion against Spain.

The next group of Creoles was made up of upwardly mobile petite bourgeoisie. Storekeepers, small landowners, businessmen, administrators for absentee landlords, independent muleteers, government employees, and parish priests in the more impoverished areas, they had enough wealth and education to desire a better deal, but not enough influence to secure it. Not far below them in social position were the self-employed artisans—either Creole or mestizo in the broadest sense—who owned the equipment with which they worked. Alongside them were the occupants of the lowest government positions such as postal clerks and night watchmen and the unemployed Creoles who would rather beg from better-placed relatives than rub shoulders with the working poor.

A final group in the cities was formed by the workers themselves, employees of the large government-owned cigar and cigarette factory, journeymen employed by artisans, street vendors, servants, and the permanently or temporarily unemployed. Especially in Mexico City, many were recent immigrants from the countryside who, no matter how bad the living conditions they encountered, knew they were better off than those they had left behind in rural areas, who faced a short supply of land for a rising population. The castas, as we have noted, were those in urban and rural areas who, along with Indians, were obliged to pay the tribute, or head tax. Some mestizos paid the tribute and some did not, thus intensifying the restlessness provoked by their unsure status.

The Indians in the central valley of Mexico and even more so those in the highland region south of Mexico City—that is, the areas of the pre-Columbian "high" civilizations—had succeeded in continuing their village life much as it had been at the time of their conquest. They had successfully resisted any massive encroachment upon their common lands, although of course many Creole-owned haciendas had been established in their midst. They were compelled to pay to the king's appointed delegate the tribute levied on each village collectively according to the number of males in a specified age bracket. Centuries of attrition had, of course, changed many ancient villages. The chieftains had become the creatures of the Spanish; the sexual appetites of the whites who passed through villages (despite royal prohibitions) had produced mestizos; and the visits of the parish priest had cast a new layer of form and meaning over the old religious practices; but the Indians still dressed in traditional clothes, spoke their ancient languages, preserved the bedrock of their spiritual life, and did not think of themselves as "Indians" but as Mixtecs or Zapotecs, that is, speakers of a common language, or as belonging to particular village communities.

In the area around Guanajuato and especially southeast of it, however, the situation was quite different. This area had never really been Aztec territory, and the Spanish presence had more easily disrupted village life. The wealth of the mines and the heightened demand for food had also tended to destroy the ancient relationships of people to land and of people to each other. The Indians understood Spanish or even spoke it, formed part of an active money economy, and often worked for wages in the city, in the mines, or on farms. They knew they did not benefit from the prosperity of the region, especially as population growth outstripped the meager lands to which Indian villages had been relegated. Many of their neighbors were mestizo small farmers.

In the neighboring region of Guadalajara similar pressures were present. The villages there were stronger, but in the face of increasing population more and more villagers were forced to leave the communal lands and seek employment on nearby estates. Estates also competed with these villages even for the use of marginal lands, for the burgeoning demand for foodstuffs in the rapidly growing city of Guadalajara meant that land had become an increasingly scarce commodity. Social and ethnic tensions particularly characterized these two regions on the eve of independence.

In the northern ranch country the life of the Indians had been even more affected by the Spaniards; they were cowhands and peons, kept in a lowly position and mixing with poor mestizos. Beyond them, in the hills of the northwest and the plains of the far north, warlike Indian tribes, almost entirely untouched by the Spanish presence except for the use of horses, pushed steadily southward.

Thus Mexico included many diverse elements. Not only were there the two broad categories of the ambitious and the satisfied, but the ambitious saw their future in diverse ways. The nouveaux riches hoped for increased wealth under a system monopolized by themselves; the mestizos wanted to participate more fully in the wealth-producing opportunities. The Indians hoped for little but revenge.

Comparisons

The diversified economy of Mexico meant that all regions would profit from closer contact with the industrial centers of Europe. The coastal planters welcomed smugglers; the mine owners were glad to get more in exchange for their product; and the nouveaux riches and petite bourgeoisie felt the future lay with them and that closer European contacts would be good. In this Mexico resembled Venezuela, which had become prominent in the first place only as the expansion of the European economy stimulated plantation agriculture and where the lure of commercial freedom attracted many. On the other hand, and not surprisingly, Spanish merchants in Mexico and Venezuela frowned equally on such a prospect.

The promise of a fluid social structure had a more varied appeal. Mexican Creoles were too aware of their past traditions and their life was too closely identified with the corporate society to abandon it that easily, so the intellectuals' influence was relatively limited, whereas Venezuelan Creoles saw no conflict between the Enlightenment's worldview and their aspirations; thus in Venezuela the new ideology spread more easily.

Venezuela and Mexico most resembled each other in the intensity of class feeling. Although the social structure of Venezuela was less complicated than that of Mexico, a similar friction between Creoles and less favored groups characterized it. The pardos of Venezuela and the mestizos of Mexico desired a more open society in which social mobility would be easier. The more acculturated Indians in the region around Guanajuato and Guadalajara in Mexico apparently felt the same way, but those of the more traditional Indian villages wished only to be left alone. Class friction would play an equally large part in the struggles for independence in Mexico and Venezuela, but in almost opposite ways, as we shall see. The contrast is even sharper if we look to Brazil and Peru, where social tensions clearly cooled the elite's ardor for independence.

Peru

At first sight it may seem odd to compare Peru with Brazil as we are about to do. The towering Andes have no counterpart in the geological formation of Brazil. The Spaniards had found the Indians in the Andes to be highly sophisticated creators of complex and densely populated civilizations, while in contrast the Portuguese had found relatively few and only nomadic Indians in Brazil. The Portuguese had thus turned to African slaves to supply the labor of the colony. There is, however, one marked similarity between these two areas that concerns us: The elites of both colonies were relatively satisfied with their colonial status.

The coastal area of Peru is arid, but along the snow-fed rivers which flow to the Pacific, plantations were established, worked by African slaves and Indian laborers. The chief crops produced on these estates were grains, cotton, and sugar, but the area was not Europe-oriented. Most production supplied only local demands and those of the highland mines, because Europe was far away and exportation difficult from Peru's location.

The wealthy landowners lived in Lima, an aristocratic, Spanish-oriented, commercial town with no roots in Indian tradition. Silver from the mines was exported through the adjoining port of Callao, and before the trade reform of 1778 all legally imported manufactured goods from Europe destined for southern Colombia, Ecuador, interior Peru, Bolivia, Argentina, and Chile had to pass through this port and the warehouses of the merchant guild's members. There were some craft shops, but most textile weaving was carried on in the northern highland city of Cajamarca. Lima, being a seat of a viceroyalty, also housed a large Spanish bureaucracy, and many of its residents were Spaniards. Most of the city's elite, whether born in Spain or America, were royal employees.

That Lima—to become practically the last center of Spanish power in America—was one of the centers of Enlightenment thought in the last part of the eighteenth century is just one more proof that ideas alone did not make the revolutions of Spanish America. A whole generation of articulate liberals studied at the Real Convictorio de San Carlos, a college-seminary created after the expulsion of the Jesuits in 1767. But these intellectuals aimed at reform, not revolution.

This limited program may be a tribute to their realism, for no groups in Lima stood to benefit from independence. Export markets were of no interest. The legal restrictions on commerce benefited the chief personages of the city, and independence could only diminish the orbit of their economic power. And the Creole aristocracy certainly preferred the glow of viceregal splendor and the ancient tradition of colonial preeminence to the crass authority of any envisioned president. The elite *limeños* (residents of Lima) had two complaints: first, that the Bourbons had taken Alto Peru, today Bolivia, out of their jurisdiction and placed it with its rich silver mines in the new Viceroyalty of Río de la Plata (albeit still leaving some newer and exceedingly productive mines in Lima's orbit); second, that the Bourbons had allowed Buenos Aires and other ports to trade directly with Spain and no longer only through Lima. To be sure, they would also have preferred lower taxes, more local control, and more freedom to exploit the Indians, that is, the revocation of most Bourbon reforms. But independence was not even thought of. Their desire was to return to a better past, not to move on to the future.

The big fear among whites, whether Creole or Spanish-born, was that the Indians would revolt. Indians made up 60 percent of the population of Peru, while "pure" whites accounted for only 12 percent. Even in Lima the whites were outnumbered by Indians, mestizos, free pardos, and slaves by a ratio of two to one. The highlands were chiefly populated by Indians of ancient civilization and depressed status, many of whom worked for minimum pay as draft laborers in the silver mines. Sometimes the Indians did revolt, most notably in the rebellion led by Tupac Amaru in 1780. José Gabriel Condorcanqui Noguera, despite his mestizo origin, claimed descent from an Inca (that is, king). He had acquired an education and became incensed at the plight of the Indian masses. Assuming the name of the last known Inca, Tupac Amaru, he called for a general rebellion in the highlands to force reform. He demanded the end of forced labor, the suspension of the most oppressive taxes, and the freedom of slaves. Bloody massacres followed in which the Indians vented upon their white oppressors the rage they had contained for centuries. But Tupac

Amaru hesitated to attack the ancient city of Cuzco, an essential target, and the Spanish authorities, recovering from their initial surprise, put down the Indian uprising within six months. Some one hundred thousand persons lost their lives. Punishment of the leaders was wreaked with unrestrained violence. The arms and legs of Tupac Amaru were tied to four horses, and he was torn apart. Other rebellions of an even more radical type then broke out in Bolivia, but they too were defeated. After peace had been restored, some attention was temporarily given to ameliorating the condition of the Indians. The rebellion frightened Creole men of property away from any revolutionary inclinations they might have otherwise developed. For, even aside from overt revolt, the Creoles knew that the Indian majority seethed with discontent.

The cities in the highland regions, where a small Spanish-speaking minority ruled over the mass of Indians, were not seriously stirred by any talk of economic injustices imposed upon them by the Spanish system. Closer contacts with northern Europe were of no interest. Curiously, however, the city of Chuquisaca (today Sucre) was the site of a university with a surprisingly advanced curriculum. The transforming spirit implicit in Enlightenment ideas made rapid advances, and some leaders of the independence movement in Buenos Aires were trained there.

But regardless of the ideas of a few intellectuals, the basic position of the Creoles of the Andean region was one of satisfaction with colonial status. Neither closer economic ties with northern Europe nor a changed society was attractive to them. There were sources of dissatisfaction, but not necessarily with colonial status. The elites would have preferred to go back to the way things were before the Bourbon reforms. Only military force brought in from outside was to effect the independence of these areas.

Brazil

REGIONS   Although Brazil is not cut up by towering mountain ranges, its vast size has exerted almost as divisive a force as the more spectacular topography of Spanish America, creating many diverse regions. The oldest area of settlement was a narrow strip of land running from the tip of the northeastern bulge southward beyond Salvador and ranging in width from fifty to one hundred miles. This area is characterized by a generally rolling terrain, a humid climate, and a rich soil, and the land was divided into sugar plantations where thousands of African slaves labored in the fields and in the mills. The masters, however, did not typically resort to sumptuous living in the cities; they preferred the placid existence of the country, where, as lord of the manor, they held overwhelming power over the slaves, their families, and other dependents. From 1550 to 1650 this region was the major supplier of sugar to the world. When mines were discovered in the region around Ouro Preto at the end of the seventeenth century, the sugar planters had to share with others their position at the center of the Brazilian economic and political stage. Although a century later they regained some of their former economic prosperity, they never regained their political importance because the revitalized Portuguese bureaucracy curtailed them. The hinterland of this coastal strip is a semiarid region and was sparsely inhabited, mostly by cowboys devoted to cattle raising.

The area to the north and west of the eastward bulge played a very small role in determining the course of affairs. Aside from a momentarily vigorous cotton production in the area near São Luís, this whole area at that time was only marginally related to the international economy. Because of the prevailing winds, communication between it and the rest of Brazil was difficult, and for long periods the area was separately administered.

The connection between the sugar coast and the south was closer, not only because of the sea, but also because the São Francisco River, which runs through the center of the hinterland, flimsily linked Salvador and Recife to the area of "General Mines," or Minas Gerais, around Ouro Preto. At the end of the seventeenth century vast resources of gold and then diamonds were discovered there, rapidly upsetting the regional, economic, and social balance of the entire colony. Many planters with their slaves abandoned everything and flocked to the region. Others came in such numbers from overseas that the Portuguese government, fearing depopulation, was forced to prohibit emigration. Around the placer mines large towns grew up overnight, overshadowing the older cities. The turbulent, socially mobile existence of these newcomers shattered old relationships. After the middle of the eighteenth century the mines played out, and the area entered a period of economic decline. The fact that so much of the mineral wealth had gone to Portugal either as taxes or as profits to Portuguese merchants made this area the scene of some discontent. As noted, an abortive conspiracy was even organized in 1789 to declare independence and establish a republic. Although supported only by a handful of conspirators, the move was symptomatic of local sentiment.

The mines had been discovered by mestizo explorers emanating from São Paulo. Driven by economic necessity, these restless, ambitious, footloose men had then extended Portuguese control over the bulk of the area that is now Brazil, despite the legal rights of Spain. At the end of the colonial period the inhabitants of São Paulo were still proud of their role in handing over to the king such vast areas and great treasures and were still resentful of the scant appreciation they had been shown in return. The regions they had opened up had been cut away from their jurisdiction, the wealth they had discovered had fallen into the hands of new arrivals from other parts of the country or from Portugal, and their free-and-easy style of self-government (or anarchy) had been circumscribed by the imposition of more stringent governmental institutions.

The discovery of the mines had drawn the political center of gravity southward, and in the 1760s the capital of the entire colony was relocated from Salvador to Rio de Janeiro. By the beginning of the nineteenth century Rio de Janeiro was the most important town on the Brazilian coast, profiting from its position as chief entrepôt for the legal and illegal commerce of the mining region. Despite its beautiful setting among green hills and sandy coves, the town of Rio de Janeiro was a backward provincial capital, beset by disease and characterized by muddy, filthy streets. Even the elevation of the colonial governor to the titular position of viceroy had not done much to give Rio de Janeiro the luster of Lima or Mexico City.

To the far south, in an area long disputed with the Spanish, lay the grasslands of Rio Grande do Sul. Life here resembled life in Uruguay or Argentina much more than life in Minas Gerais. Yet its inhabitants conceived of themselves as Portuguese and increasingly as Brazilians.

Among Brazil's various regions, no single one achieved complete preeminence. Its configuration has been described as that of an archipelago. Most governors reported directly to the king in Lisbon and not through the viceroy. As a result, in Brazil before 1808 one does not find the same tension, competition, and rivalry as existed between Montevideo and Buenos Aires or Chile and Peru, that is, between lesser provinces and a predominant center. These would come only later.

GROUPS   The Creole[3] sugar planters were satisfied with their colonial status, for the Portuguese were relatively lax in administration and the elite had a great deal of political power to add to their wealth. They not only ruled unchecked over their vast slave-worked properties, they also dominated the câmaras, or municipal county councils. The centralizing effort to create a national state, ably directed by the marquis of Pombal, did begin to trim the wings of local câmaras; but the new program was not enforced overnight, and the Creoles' irritation remained minimal. Furthermore, not only did the Portuguese not restrict commerce as severely as the Spanish did, but since England protected Jamaican sugar by placing a high tariff on the Brazilian product, the major market for Brazil was the Continent, and Portugal was a natural entrepôt. And the sugar planters, unlike a few leaders in the mining regions, did not care that there were prohibitions on manufacturing. Planters and miners alike, however, resented the wealth and prominence of Portuguese merchants in the coastal towns.

Excluded from immediate landownership because of their late arrival and initially limited resources and refusing to work as farmhands alongside slaves, the Portuguese immigrants had tended to concentrate in commerce. Landowners disdained this activity and at first successfully prevented the merchants from sitting on the local câmaras. But, as the Portuguese merchants prospered, they became the creditors of the landowners, and real animosity sprang up between the two groups. If the children of these immigrants decided to stay in Brazil, they bought plantations themselves or foreclosed on mortgages and moved as quickly as possible to disassociate themselves from the activity of their fathers. Just as often, the immigrant or his son returned to Portugal to enjoy the fruits of hard labor and the rewards for enduring the scorn of the planters. These merchants naturally wanted the government to intensify the restrictions laid

---

[3] For the sake of simplicity, I will use the familiar term "Creole" to refer to any person of entirely Spanish or Portuguese descent born in America despite the fact that in Brazil the term *crioulo* meant a black person born in America.

upon trade with foreigners. They also cherished their monopoly of government contracts for the equipment of the navy, the collection of taxes, or the supply of stores to government establishments. The colonial relationship remained dear to them.

By the end of the eighteenth century a small lower middle class had gathered in a few cities. This class was easily stirred up against the aloof and haughty merchants. Caught between the upper grindstone of Portuguese predominance and the nether one of cheap slave labor, this class proved irritable and tense and therefore volatile. In 1798 mulatto tailors and common soldiers, led by a priest and a Latin teacher, launched an unsuccessful revolt in Salvador. Their mixed race and less-than-elite social position led to much harsher punishments than those meted out to the wealthy leaders of the 1789 conspiracy. By this time the experience of Haiti had also heightened upper-class fears of a race war.

The chief manipulators of discontent in the cities were the urban intellectuals, inspired by the ideals of the Enlightenment and devoted to the inclusion of their country in the main currents of the Western world. But their importance must not be exaggerated. There were not

Slaves Transporting a Brazilian woman

only few issues to play upon but also few intellectuals. There was no university or institution of higher education in all of Brazil, and not everyone could afford to study in Portugal. Furthermore, the fact that no printing press existed in Brazil before 1808 greatly limited the effectiveness of the intellectuals in spreading their ideas. If it had not been for extra-Brazilian events, decades would probably have passed before they could have mobilized enough favorable opinion to create an independent Brazil.

Comparisons

The failure of these innovating intellectuals suggests the real similarities between Brazil and Peru, despite the obvious differences. In both these regions those excited by the Enlightenment found few cracks of elite dissatisfaction into which to wedge new ideas, for the elite Creoles had few reasons to complain. Unlike the situation in Argentina, Venezuela, or Mexico, the trading monopoly did not irritate most Creole leaders in Brazil or Peru. And social tensions as intense as those in Mexico or Venezuela worked to dampen Creole interest in altering the old colonial system. Aside from abortive revolts stimulated by fringe elements in Bolivia, Ouro Preto, and Salvador, independence came to both Brazil and the Andean core area from outside and was not formalized until the 1820s, a full decade after independence movements began elsewhere. The elite's need to maintain control over their workers far exceeded their desire for change.

Chapter Three
Toward War

P olitical agitation in Spanish America began in 1808, when news arrived of Napoleon's usurpation of the Spanish crown, and took on real impetus as news reached America of his victories against resistance fighters in Spain. The independence movement enjoyed victories and suffered defeats until the restoration of King Ferdinand VII to the Spanish throne in 1814, after which the movement suffered mostly defeats until the 1820s; its fortunes then turned and culminated in victory in 1824. Although the course of the independence movement in Portuguese America was entirely different, related events in Europe brought about a similar result: When Napoleon invaded Portugal in 1807, the king actually fled to his American domain, which made Brazil, in a sense, independent, but not completely free of Portuguese control for another two decades and even then not without some struggle. In this chapter we will first look at the causes of independence in America and then turn to the European events that formed its context.

Tracing Cause

The independence movement in Spanish America can be divided chronologically into two distinct wars for independence.[1] The causes

---

[1] In Brazil military clashes occurred only at the time of the second war in Spanish America.

of the second war are easily found in the experiences of the first, unsuccessful one and in the behavior of the Spaniards after the revolutionaries' first defeat. The puzzle, then, is how the widely divergent regional and group reactions to the possibility of trade with England and the political and social transformations promised by Enlightenment liberalism can be linked to the onset and course of the first war. We will trace those connections by working backward from military action to the role of diverse interest groups, to the impact of ideas, and finally, to the nature of the constitutional crisis that confronted Latin Americans.

MILITARY FORCE   If Spain in 1810 and the years immediately thereafter had been able to marshal its full military might against the revolutionaries in America instead of dispatching only small reinforcements, events there might have been very different. In some areas, such as Peru, Spanish power during this initial period was never even challenged; in other places local Spanish forces were sufficient for the task at hand. A small Spanish garrison, moving out of Puerto Rico, drew upon the enthusiastic support of Creole royalists to sweep away the first independent government of Venezuela in 1812; Spanish armies, marching from Peru, expelled liberating Argentine soldiers from Bolivia in 1813 and crushed the revolutionary movement in Chile the following year. In many places the first war for independence was really a civil war. Evidently, a relatively small increase in Spanish power or an equally small decrease in insurgent strength might have eliminated all the foci of revolutionary action in America, prevented the drawn-out struggle that hardened attitudes and divided Americans from Spaniards, and maintained the Spanish Empire intact for perhaps another fifty years. Instead, the Spanish garrison in Venezuela was unable to subdue Colombia until reinforcements arrived from Spain in 1814, and the armies from Peru did not have sufficient strength to move to Buenos Aires and snuff out the movement there. In Mexico large-scale war raged continuously from 1810 to 1815. In most of the empire Spain was victorious by 1816, but it had taken too long and its success had been too incomplete. These two factors were crucial in provoking the second, successful war.

The chief military opposition to the Spanish forces in 1810 came from the Creole militia. In Buenos Aires Creole officers pressured the cabildo and the viceroy to create a local committee to rule on behalf of Ferdinand VII. In Chile the story was much the same. In Colombia the militia officers fraternized with the mobs that they were supposed to disperse. The importance of the Creole officers may be judged by the contrasting situation in Mexico: Instead of siding with the revolutionaries, many Mexican militia officers were the first to take the leadership in crushing them. The explanation is that some intellectuals and middle-class professionals there made the mistake of arousing the Indians to revolt; with all property and established social relations in jeopardy, the bulk of the wealthier Creoles sided with Spain. If the Creole officers had similarly put down the revolutionaries in other parts of Spanish America, no movement toward independence would even have begun.

The ascendancy of the Creole militia in Spanish America was short-lived, however. In Venezuela they failed to maintain the loyalty of their troops, made up of freed slaves and pardos. In Chile and Colombia they fought among themselves, opening the way for Spanish reconquest. But the point is that the Creole militia officers successfully initiated the independence movement by using the force they commanded, successfully held off the Spanish for several years in much of Spanish America, and kept Argentina completely free of Spanish domination after 1810.

INTEREST GROUPS   In view of the early importance of the Creole militia officers, the position of the aristocracy and professional middle class from which they arose is of prime importance in explaining the onset of the independence movement, but the diversity of sentiment among these classes exemplifies the complexity of Latin America. Although it is probably safe to say that in every area there were some wealthy Creoles who were willing to support independence, the strength of their feeling varied greatly.

In some regions the landowners' interest in independence was based on economic reasons. The planters of Venezuela and coastal Mexico and Colombia, and the ranchers around Buenos Aires, knew that their products were consumed in northern Europe and that they would get better prices through direct sales. But there were other regions where the economic factor was relatively unimportant. The hacendados of Chile sent their products mostly to Peru and were free to send them to other ports along the Pacific coast or to Argentina, and those of the Colombian highlands distributed their products locally because the terrain prevented them from supplying the coast. None of these landowners was interested in direct exports to overseas consuming centers. Nor did the landowners in the highlands of Mexico have any particular desire to export to northern Europe. Thus the landowners in different regions were impelled as much by economic interests as by social theory to take opposite positions regarding independence.

Nor was the advantage of the lower cost of imported manufactured goods of equal interest to all consumers, although the landowners always supported steps which facilitated this importation unless it offended their other interests. In Chile, for instance, where they were not much hurt by the old system, they were nevertheless willing to consider change. They received silver from Peru in exchange for their wheat, and this silver went farther when the prices of manufactured imports were lower. Similarly, the gold exported from Colombia paid for more manufactured goods when sent directly to England. The haciendas of highland Mexico supplied foodstuffs to the mining towns; the mineral wealth received in return went to pay for the expenses of sumptuous town houses which called for European imports. Even the hacienda itself required some tools and other iron products best supplied from abroad. On the other hand, if the imported products competed in price with local ones, then the feeling was reversed. Thus the wine and sugar producers of western Argentina looked with disfavor upon measures which opened the east coast to foreign competition; however, these producers were in the minority.

If the landowners remained loyal to Spain, this loyalty resulted most often from other kinds of countervailing pressures. Most noticeable is the case of Mexico, where the landowners perceived much more advantage in maintaining Spanish power than surrendering to what they believed to be a maddened horde of Indians. In Peru the fear was so direct that no one moved to break the tie with Spain. In Venezuela many men of property joined the struggle for independence, but conflict between them and the lower classes caused them much difficulty in their effort. And even where social tensions did not surface, it may be said that only when the desire for cheaper imports combined with other interests—a desire for better prices on exports, lower taxes generally, or greater power locally—did the landowners get stirred up enough to fight for independence.

Among merchants, distinctions must be made between those who profited from the monopoly trading system and those who did not. The former were mostly Spanish-born agents of the large merchant firms of Cádiz. Even after the trade reforms of the 1770s, large-scale legal commerce remained in their hands. In outlying areas like Santiago, Montevideo, or Guatemala City the establishment of merchant guilds symbolized the achievement of their maximum aims. Although the old, established merchants, as in Lima or Veracruz, resented the increasing freedom granted by the Bourbon kings and imposed by the turn-of-the-century wars, they did not think independence would be better than the status quo. The most that can be said is that perhaps some of them were lackadaisical in defending a system which seemed to them already destroyed.

The men who bought from the old, established merchants were often Creole middlemen. These small merchants were ambitious types, unreconciled to remaining forever in the shadow of the larger merchant houses and susceptible to the wiles of the contrabandist. When the leaders of independence movements moved to loosen the commercial system, lifting restrictions on foreign trade and ending many of the earlier monopolies, these merchants benefited and gave the new governments their support. This was true in Buenos Aires and in Caracas and would have been true in the minor cities of Mexico (for example, Veracruz) had not the independence leaders there threatened the safety of all trade. It is interesting to contrast the position of the merchants of western Argentina and Lima—who almost unanimously looked back nostalgically to better days, were far from anxious to transform Buenos Aires into an even larger entrepôt, and saw independence as a step in the same direction as the "disastrous" Bourbon reforms—with those in Mexico City, who, because of the greater vigor of its trade and the profits some had derived from the Bourbon measures, violently disagreed among themselves as to whether independence would be good or bad.

The position of craftsmen before the threat or promise of independence has not yet been adequately studied. The threat of competing foreign imports would surely have strengthened their loyalty to Spain, but many of them derived more protection from the difficulties of internal transport than from legal rigidities. The textile shops in Puebla, Mexico, seem to have helped maintain that city on the side of Spanish power until 1820; but their counterparts in Socorro,

Colombia, do not appear to have shared their loyalty. In some areas, as in southern Colombia, where craftsmen were important, one may ask whether it was direct economic interest or the highly traditional societal structure that contributed to the strength of loyalist sentiment.

Closely related to the question of trade, but in a sense overriding it, was the question of power. There is little doubt that the Creole aristocracy and professional middle class desired power and wished to wrest it from the supercilious Spanish bureaucrats. This ambition was linked to the issue of free commerce, because with power they could foster their own economic interests, whatever they were. The fulfillment of this goal would also—and this is very important—give them the right to tax and disburse funds in their own behalf. Ironically, they believed that mestizos and mulattoes could then more easily be kept in their place and also that the Indians could be further exploited, as indeed they later were.

IDEAS   The role of the Creole intellectuals assumes real importance once the position of landowners and militia is clear. Committed to change and knowing what they wanted, the intellectuals were quick to take advantage of a crisis whose origins lay in Europe, to play upon the economic or other interests of landowners, and to manipulate the officers. In Peru the intellectuals' endeavors were a failure because of the entrenched conservatism of Spanish merchants, bureaucrats, and churchmen; in Mexico their entreaties also fell upon deaf ears because of initial tactical mistakes; but in Argentina, Chile, Venezuela, and Colombia the intellectuals were successful primarily because they expounded a well-elaborated ideology.

This ideology was the Enlightenment. Some Spanish government officials considered the new doctrines then sweeping Europe to be dangerous and subversive to the established order. But their effort to prevent the penetration of these ideas proved to be a chimerical goal, for ideas have a life of their own. Once any Latin American had had contact with the new critical approach, nothing could prevent him from thinking subversive thoughts and even "infecting" others.

Antonio Nariño (1769–1822), a somewhat quixotic Colombian intellectual, demonstrates the conclusions to which the Enlightenment could lead. In 1794 he translated and published the Declaration of the Rights of Man, apparently unaware of the effect this would have upon a government fast becoming jittery over the regicidal behavior of French revolutionaries. Nariño had the curious idea that he could make money from this editorial venture despite the fact that he had to print it in the secrecy of his home. The Spanish authorities seized him and, after imprisoning him, shipped him off to Spain in chains. In the port of Cádiz, however, he escaped his ship as it was docking and proceeded disguised through Spain to France and then to England. Nariño then trustingly returned to his native land, where he was promptly clapped back into jail, to be released only in 1803 for medical reasons. He was then required to remain on his landed estate under virtual house arrest.

Preventing the distribution of a translated Declaration of the Rights of Man was one thing; preventing the spread of its ideas was quite another. Literate men were bound to discuss these ideas whenever they met. Furthermore, many societies had been formed with royal approval both in Spain and in America for the purpose of propagating novel agricultural techniques, stimulating economic activity, discussing industrial possibilities, and exploring the applicability of newly discovered scientific principles. The intellectuals who organized such clubs in Latin America and who published or wrote for periodicals to expound and popularize these new ideas found that, in order to change economic conditions and transform Spanish America into a progressive, scientifically oriented, and entrepreneurially active society, basic changes were needed in the social structure and political organization. For these intellectuals, it was not possible to speak of progress without casting a new look at tax structures, commercial restrictions, and monopoly agents. Inevitably, Spanish authorities disbanded the societies, confiscated the periodicals, questioned the leaders, and made other attempts to foster "clean" societies.

At first most of the intellectuals would have been satisfied with reform. If Spain had granted more local autonomy in 1810 or 1812, perhaps the intellectuals would not have pushed the movement to independence; but Spain did not, and independence became their goal. Although the intellectuals' subsequent efforts fell far short of a genuine bourgeois revolution, they were not entirely without fruit in moving Spanish America closer to the mainsprings of Europe. The patterns of society and economy were far different in 1830 than in 1808. This result was due partly to the influence of ideas.

CONSTITUTIONAL CRISIS   The ideas of the intellectuals would have been in vain—or at least long delayed in their effect—if it had not been for the unsettling events that overtook Spanish America entirely without local effort: In Europe Napoleon usurped the Spanish throne. This event created a crisis because of the preexisting constitution of the Spanish-American government. Conceivably, Spanish Americans could have continued to obey viceroys, audiencias, and intendants; and they could have received instructions from the Spaniards who had fought against Napoleon; but, although this policy was adopted in some places, it was rejected in most because Spanish Americans did not consider themselves colonials. Napoleon had removed their *own* king, usurped his throne, and left them entirely without a government. Without a king, where did one's loyalty lie? The ties that bound a man to his own home were the only other worthwhile emotional commitment. With the king gone, only the immediate locality remained. Thus the regionalism that has so often been decried as the tragedy of the Spanish-American wars of independence was, in fact, their very root.

When the Spanish failed to recognize the validity of this regionalist sentiment and autonomist impulse, attempting instead to enforce their rule, the Creole elite resisted. The old animosities between those born in Spain and those born in America came to the surface. The intellectuals provided justifications and suggested alternative forms of government that could be useful, and the militia provided the necessary armed force to initiate the war. Except in Venezuela (and to some extent in Mexico), the first movements did not aim at independence. A considered program and definite goals were hewed out only during the course of warfare against "illegitimate" Spanish pretenders and years of self-governing experience. Meanwhile, new groups that had never been heard from before emerged to prominence and had to be taken into account. The old system could certainly not be reimposed on them. So the causes of the Second War of Independence (after 1815) are different from those operative from 1808 to 1810. Although pressures toward independence would probably have surfaced eventually, the timing of these wars resulted from European events.

European Events

SPAIN AND FRANCE, 1788–1805   The "enlightened despot" Charles III of Spain died just a year before the French Revolution broke out. His successor, Charles IV (reigned 1788–1808), was well-meaning but stupid and did whatever his wife wished. At middle age her fancy turned to romance with a handsome if overweight twenty-five-year-old officer in the palace guard. Manuel Godoy (1767–1851) was of petit bourgeois background; he thought he was a liberal, but he was primarily an opportunist. As the queen's favorite, Godoy was rapidly promoted not only into her bedchamber but also to the post of chief minister of the realm. Charles IV gave him full powers over domestic and foreign policies, and Godoy became a mean and petty dictator. The old aristocrats were outraged at this climber's success, and the reformers were appalled to see such a charlatan pretending to their principles.

With the leftward swing of France after 1789, Spanish leaders became steadily more frightened. Spain abandoned its historic enmity toward England and in 1791 temporarily joined her in the First Coalition against France. By late 1793, however, this coalition began to fall apart. The end of the Terror in France and the assumption of power by the more conservative Directorate assuaged Spanish fears and made an alliance with England distasteful. France and Spain therefore signed a treaty of friendship in 1796. When Russia and England formed a Second Coalition against France in 1798, Spain preferred to side with France, and England, whose navy completely controlled the seas, retaliated by cutting Spain off from her American colonies. The year before, the Spanish government had officially sanctioned colonial trade with friendly neutrals; and although this trade was envisioned to be with the United States, it was the British who reaped the greatest advantage from such liberality. This measure gave the colonials the experience of economic independence: The trade of Veracruz tripled in one year. When the government revoked this permission two years later, English vessels continued illegally to ply the Spanish coast in the Caribbean, in the Río de la Plata region, and on the west coast of South America. With the resumption of war between Spain and England in 1803, Spanish commerce to America was entirely cut off for long periods and neutral trade became the norm. Thus the economic independence of the colonies was being forged long before political independence became a live issue.

The alliance between France and Spain continued after Napoleon's rise to power. In 1801 he played upon the silly pride of the fawning Spanish royalty by promising to give a kingdom in Italy to the daughter of Charles IV in exchange for that part of Louisiana which Spain had been granted at the conclusion of the Seven Years' War. Then French armies joined Spanish ones in attacking Portugal, England's protégé. Portugal yielded part of its own territory to Spain and allowed French Guiana to expand southward to the mouth of the Amazon River. A further threat to annex all of Portugal ended with the signing in 1802 of the Treaty of Amiens between France and England. According to its terms England was allowed to keep Trinidad, which it had captured from the Spanish in 1797 and had consistently used as a base for clandestine trade with Spanish America, and France was left with its new territories in Louisiana and Brazil, both controlling access to continental river systems and both well situated in relation to the Caribbean. But Napoleon's refusal to accept the British demand for a cessation of his expansionist activities on the Continent was unsatisfactory to the British, who declared war the next year.

Napoleon was taken by surprise. He now concentrated on Europe. Louisiana was hastily sold to the United States, and despite Spain's disappointment at this act, she was persuaded to declare war on England. For Napoleon had decided to invade England and needed additional Spanish ships to transport men and equipment across the channel. But the French and Spanish fleets were hounded into port at Cádiz; when they attempted to break out, Lord Nelson decisively defeated them off Cape Trafalgar in 1805.

SPAIN AND ENGLAND, 1797–1807   If Napoleon could readily discard or postpone his overseas ambitions, British policy makers faced a more difficult choice: Should they concentrate on colonial conquests, leaving the Continental war to their allies? Or should they concentrate on defeating the French in Europe, in the face of their allies' failure of will and inability to fight to the end? Instead of making a firm choice, the British pursued an ambivalent policy that did much to foster independence sentiment in Spanish America but not enough to accomplish independence.

The difficulty of resolving this dilemma was not only strategic but political and economic: The business community was in desperate straits. The newly mechanized factories were producing more products than the markets were able to absorb. The years of war with France had broken old commercial ties on the Continent, and the Treaty of Amiens had failed to restore them, while it had simultaneously curtailed trade in Spanish America. If the Spanish colonies could be captured, the business community would have a sure market and the government would have a secure source of bullion to finance the allies. But England lacked the resources for a massive colonial war; the only alternative was to encourage revolution, for the English had not forgotten the American Revolution; nor had Francisco de Miranda.

Miranda (1750–1817) was born in Venezuela and went to Spain as a young man to join the army. He fought against the British in the American Revolution, which the Spanish and the French supported. Although he did not think much of the United States, Miranda somewhere absorbed liberal ideas and a belief in colonial freedom. He eventually abandoned the Spanish army and roamed Europe seeking support for his schemes to free Spanish America. He found that the London business community and also the naval captain Sir Home Popham were interested in his plans. Popham introduced Miranda to his influential political friends, a step which ultimately led to semiofficial conversations with William Pitt. These conversations resulted in a plan to invade Venezuela with a few thousand troops. But the plan was abruptly halted when Pitt was persuaded that Spain could still be won away from France and included in a Third Coalition, but obviously not if England aided a movement aimed at independence in Spain's colonies. Miranda in disgust departed England and headed for the United States, and Popham was dispatched to capture the Cape of Good Hope from the Dutch before it could become unfriendly territory. Neither Miranda nor Popham forgot the possibility of liberating Spanish America.

Miranda, doggedly determined to carry on without British support, obtained two hundred men and sailed out of New York for Venezuela in January 1806. He was so completely out of touch with affairs in his home country that he thought his mere appearance off the coast of Venezuela would result in an uprising. Instead, when he landed in April, the local inhabitants stared at him uncomprehendingly and

Spanish forces quickly routed him. Miranda sailed for the West Indies, where he secured the promise of support from British Admiral Thomas Cochrane. Thus encouraged, Miranda tried again without success. The British cabinet received the news of his attempts at the same time as it was trying to arrange peace with France. An attack on Spanish colonies seemed ill timed, but the cabinet instructed Cochrane to send "full details of the situation in which the Continent of South America now stands."[2]

Meanwhile, Popham became bored with his duty of patrolling the Atlantic around the Cape of Good Hope. He heard that Napoleon had smashed the Third Coalition at Austerlitz in December 1805. Since this assured Spain's loyalty to France, Popham assumed that Pitt had given him authority to take such measures against the Spanish as he and Miranda had once imagined. In April 1806 Popham set off for the Río de la Plata region with part of an army garrison commanded by William Carr Beresford to capture either Montevideo or Buenos Aires. News that Buenos Aires had just received a shipment of silver from the interior decided him in its favor. The city was captured almost without effort. But a Creole militia, led by Juan Martín de Pueyrredón, drove the British out of the city in August.

Beresford in the meantime had sent home not only news of the initial success but also over $1 million in booty, which was paraded through the commercial section of London in September. The merchants were electrified. In 1805 their exports to Spanish and Portuguese America had amounted to more than $38 million; they felt that if this trade could be relieved of the frightening fluctuations which accompanied its illegality, there was no telling how high the figure would reach. The merchants rushed to send out goods on consignment to Buenos Aires and pressured the British government to support their enterprise with guns.

Some members of the British cabinet had been advocating a more forceful Latin American policy all along. Now, as had not been the case with Miranda's adventure, a British force had been successful, even if unauthorized, and must be supported. Also, Napoleon's victories and his decrees closing Europe to British trade affected the decision. So a military force was sent out to reinforce Popham, and

---

[2] Quoted by William Spence Robertson, *The Life of Miranda*, 2 vols. (Chapel Hill: University of North Carolina Press, 1929), vol. I, p. 318.

plans were made for attacks on Panamá, Chile, Peru, the Philippines, and Mexico.

Inefficiency, red tape, and the difficulty of preparing concrete plans delayed action; then, in January 1807, news arrived that the British forces had been forced out of Buenos Aires the previous August. The grand plan was reduced to concentrating on recapturing Buenos Aires. Yet even in this modest aim the British were unsuccessful. Although an army of ten thousand men was dispatched to Buenos Aires, it was met with fierce house-to-house combat in which the British suffered a thousand casualties and lost two thousand prisoners. A truce was struck, and by September 1807 the defeated British were on their way home. The militia, led by upper- and middle-class Creoles and manned by Creoles and mestizos of all classes, had won again. The British defeat indicated that Spanish Americans were not eagerly awaiting their deliverance from Spain.

PORTUGAL, 1807–1808   News of this debacle reached London only a few months before the announcement of Napoleon's pact with the Russian czar at Tilsit. Napoleon now dominated practically all of Europe, and he intended to enclose the remainder. He was furious at Portugal for not closing its ports to British trade even though he knew that his armies were often dependent on British goods smuggled through those ports. In mid-August 1807 Napoleon demanded that Portugal declare war on England and join the Continental system. For Portugal there were three alternatives. One was to yield to Napoleon's demands. But if Portugal declared war on England, that would be the end of her domination in Brazil because England controlled the sea. Another possibility was for Portugal to join England. England, however, demanded that Portugal remove her restrictions upon British penetration of the Brazilian market—Britain's economic plight was intensified by Napoleon's closing the European ports—and that the Portuguese court be moved to Brazil for safety. The third possibility was for Portugal delicately to play France against England, desperately trying to save through sophisticated diplomacy what Portugal's limited military capability could not hope to safeguard. Negotiations were spun out so that Napoleon's ultimatum requiring compliance by September 1, 1807, was not carried to its conclusion until late November. In the meantime Portugal attempted to persuade England to agree to a false declaration of war, but England found this duplicity distasteful and was too anxious to get the Brazilian trade to play that game. At the beginning of November Portugal began to comply outwardly with Napoleon's demands while keeping England informed of every step.

The Portuguese leaders carefully outlined another course of action in case these steps failed. This contingency plan consisted of moving the court, government, and accouterments of government to Brazil. Every detail was foreseen. Bureaucrats secretly surveyed and charted all the ships to measure available space; established a line of command; selected papers; put treasury accounts into order. But they took no overt action because any sign that the government indeed planned to flee, as the British desired, would have provoked an invasion. Only one problem could not be overcome: Portugal's small size meant that an invasion could be known in Lisbon only four days before French armies would arrive at the city. The Portuguese gambled that this would be enough time to carry out the massive task of removing not just the sovereign but the entire machinery of government. They won that gamble. Only the sails of the ships were visible when Napoleon's officers reached the Lisbon quay in late November 1807.

The careful planning that enabled the Portuguese government to escape French domination is all the more impressive because the court in Brazil was to be not simply a government in exile, but a new empire. On the ships traveled the prince regent (later King John VI); his mother, the queen, who was mentally incapacitated; his wife, Carlota, who was the sister of Ferdinand VII and would soon dream of replacing him as sovereign in Spanish America; her young sons, Pedro and Miguel; and other members of the royal family. The cabinet, several layers of the bureaucracy, judges, and the upper clergy, joined at the last minute by their friends and friends of their friends, also went aboard. Fifteen thousand Portuguese crowded into ships that had been prepared for one-third that many.

The crossing of the Atlantic was not easy. The escorting British ships could not prevent the onslaught of a storm that scattered the vessels and greatly delayed their arrival. Food and water ran short. By the time the Portuguese sighted the Brazilian coast in early 1808, the women had been forced to shave their heads to rid themselves of lice; the wives of the Brazilian planters who flocked to the port to greet them thought this must be the latest fashion in Europe and hastened to do likewise.

On arrival in Brazil, the Portuguese government's first action was to throw open the ports of Brazil to the trade of friendly nations. British merchants now had at their disposal a market of 2 million people to be clothed with cottons made in British mills. Napoleon's action had done more for British businessmen than Popham's or Miranda's.

SPAIN, 1807–1814   Thus encouraged, British leaders looked once again at the prospects in Spanish America. In early 1808 Arthur Wellesley was charged with studying the military aspects of a campaign to liberate Venezuela. Wellesley concluded that conquest was out of the question, but that, if the Venezuelans desired it, liberation was within the realm of possibility. The British recalled Miranda from his virtual exile in the West Indies and assured him that at last his hopes were to be realized: Britain would free Spanish America from Spanish "oppression." But his hopes were soon shattered once again.

For at this point Napoleon decided to take direct control of Spain. He had already cajoled Godoy into allowing French troops to cross Spain to reach Portugal and had then established a corridor across Spain between France and Portugal. The old aristocrats continued to chafe at Godoy's crass behavior and looked to Prince Ferdinand, who was old enough to think for himself (which does not mean he did so), for salvation. They hoped he would lead a revolt against his father. When Napoleon demanded the right to occupy northern Spain, officers in the army, supported by a skillfully manipulated mob in the streets, successfully demanded the abdication of Charles IV. Then in May 1808 Napoleon lured both Charles IV and Ferdinand VII to southern France under the pretext of offering mediation, but instead he announced that Charles's abdication would hold and that Ferdinand would abdicate in behalf of Napoleon's brother Joseph Bonaparte. Offered the choice between a risky attempt at escape, perhaps to America, and the gift of a comfortable estate in France, Ferdinand chose the latter.

No sooner did news spread that Ferdinand had been kidnapped than revolts broke out in Spain, driving Joseph from Madrid. Only massive military support from France was able to restore him to the capital. Then began the Spanish War of Independence. Like the wars that subsequently swept Spanish America, it was also a civil war. Many Spaniards had always looked to France for their inspiration and felt that a new king could perhaps revitalize Spain as the Bourbons had done a century before. The Spaniards who thus collaborated with the foreigner were mostly moderate liberals. This collaboration with the foreigner helped discredit liberalism in Spain throughout the nineteenth century. The opponents of the French were either conservatives or ultraliberal nationalists and naturally fell to quarreling.

Nevertheless, the French found it hard going. Juntas, or committees, were organized to direct defense efforts in each Spanish province and each village. These juntas quickly turned to guerrilla warfare. In this the Spanish proved highly effective as it places a premium on individual action, courage, mobility, and the commitment of the population. Furthermore, guerrilla warfare (the word originated at this time and place) puts a regular army to its hardest test because in its desperation the regulars alienate the civilian population, whose disaffection provides the basis for guerrilla success. Napoleon soon complained that Spain was like a running sore. He had to pour thousands of French troops in to hold territory, for as soon as a French army moved on to another target after capturing one locality the Spaniards rose up again and fought from the rear. Still, Napoleon did manage little by little to expand the area under his control.

The first British reaction to Napoleon's move on Spain was to think of Spanish America. Wellesley was appointed commander of an army to invade it. But when delegates from rebel juntas in Spain arrived in England and told of the fierce struggle that the French still faced, it seemed to the British that the best policy was to help them. So they sent Wellesley to Spain instead. In such a situation it was impossible openly to encourage revolution in Spanish America; yet it was equally foolish to discourage it in case the peninsular campaign failed.

In September 1808 the various Spanish juntas sent representatives to a coordinating committee in Seville, out of which developed the Central Junta. Two years later this junta fled further southward to Cádiz, where it could be protected by the British navy. In February 1810 the Central Junta in desperation dissolved itself to be replaced by a five-man regency ruling on behalf of the king. In quest of legitimacy (for Napoleon pointed to Ferdinand's signed abdication and a constitution promulgated by Joseph Bonaparte as the basis for his), this regency summoned a *cortes*, or parliament, to meet in Cádiz in September, 1810.

Most members of the cortes were young radicals. The moderate liberals were collaborating with the French, and the conservatives were too attached to their properties or their responsibilities to run from the French. Only the radicals were free enough of material and moral encumbrances to flee to Cádiz. Although representatives were to be elected in every region, the areas under French control were represented by anyone in Cádiz from that place. In their deliberations the members of the Cortes sought to outbid Napoleon in their adherence to Enlightenment ideas on politics and society. The result was the liberal Constitution of 1812, which established a constitutional monarchy that so restrained the power of the king that it was virtually a republic. Power would reside in a parliament chosen, albeit indirectly, by the people. All cabildos would henceforth be fully elective bodies, and provincial deputations would also be elected to advise administrative agents (including viceroys and captains-general in the colonies) on the exercise of their duties, replacing the audiencias, which would now serve only as courts of law. Such measures were implemented only fitfully in the colonies, but such elections as were held gave Spanish Americans their first taste of representative government. Moreover, by abolishing many of the institutions of the old regime—press censorship, the Inquisition, privileges of the nobility, feudal dues, the fueros—these constitution makers uttered a cry of ultraliberalism that reverberated throughout Spanish America for more than a decade.

On only one issue did the Cortes shy away from change: The colonies were to remain dependent. In Cádiz, the very center of the monopoly trade which characterized colonial relations, the monopoly merchants who financed the insurgent effort were naturally influential. Even though virtually no Spanish ships could actually sail to America, when the British demanded that the ports of America be legally opened, Spanish leaders replied that their efforts in fighting the French were a sufficient sacrifice for the cause. Although the regency issued a call for delegates to the Cortes from the colonies (to be chosen by the cabildos in all provincial capitals), it made sure that these delegates, even in the unlikely event they all came and arrived in time for the deliberations, would be outvoted. In the absence of the colonial delegates Americans resident in Cádiz filled some of the American seats. Delegates who did arrive joined in asking for greater colonial autonomy and the end of the monopoly trading system, but on both counts they were ignored. The Cortes majority thought themselves generous in accepting all residents of the colonies as part of the "Spanish nation," whereas what those colonials wanted was to be separate nations, albeit within a kind of Spanish commonwealth.

Meanwhile, the military struggle was beginning to go against the French. Wellesley's army slowly consolidated its hold in Spain and occupied more territory. At the end of 1812 the French armies were also forced to retreat from Russia; the next year they suffered further defeats by a Fourth Coalition of anti-French allies and were also driven out of Spain. In the spring of 1814 allied armies converged on Paris.

Napoleon released Ferdinand VII on the startling condition that he restore the Spanish-French alliance. By the time Ferdinand occupied his throne in March 1814, there really was no Napoleonic government left. In May Ferdinand tore up the Constitution of 1812 and proceeded to persecute both those who had collaborated with the French and the radicals who had dominated the Cortes. He, like the French Bourbons, had forgotten nothing and learned nothing.

Chapter Four

The First War of Independence

The First War of Independence was directly provoked by the constitutional crisis in Spain. Creole intellectuals committed to social and political change, economic elites interested in forging closer commercial relationships with northern Europe, or both, seized the moment to gain control of the juntas that had been set up in a number of Spanish-American centers to deal with that crisis. These leaders enjoyed momentary success but were eventually defeated by internal divisions and crushed by Spanish forces. By 1815 or 1816 peninsulars were in control of all of Latin America except Argentina and Paraguay. Yet despite the defeats that marked the conclusion of this First War of Independence, it is the more important war for it clearly established the issues and created the sentiments that would prove decisive in the second war. It also exposed the terribly sharp internal divisions that have characterized Latin America ever since.

Argentina

The British invasions of Buenos Aires in 1806 and 1807 encouraged a closer connection between the Río de la Plata region and northern

Europe. Landowners, ranchers, small merchants, and intellectuals were excited by the possibilities opened up by direct commercial connections, and the alleviation of customs dues under the British further emphasized the burdensome nature of Spanish rule. Moreover, the Creoles were encouraged by the militia's victory over a well-trained and experienced European army and by their heady experience, when the Spanish appointee fled, of choosing their own viceroy, Jacques "Santiago" de Liniers. The British invasions, therefore, are justifiably looked back upon as a turning point in the road toward independence in Argentina, even though the British themselves were sent packing.

In January 1809 Creole troops turned back an attempt by Spanish merchants to remove Liniers, and the government in Spain, racked by crises there, did not send out a replacement for him until the middle of that year. The new viceroy who arrived in Buenos Aires was named not by the king, but by the Central Junta of Seville. His claim to rule was based on the theory that these American provinces were part of Spain, not merely joint kingdoms under a common crown, and that the Central Junta was therefore the only legitimate representative of the king. He was uneasily accepted. His most immediate task was to solve the economic problem. With Spain largely occupied by foreign troops and the normal channels of trade closed, the Creole landowners, ranchers, and small merchants stridently demanded that in the present crisis they be allowed to trade freely with all countries. The intellectuals, most notably Mariano Moreno, readily provided for their use reasoned arguments based on Enlightenment thought. The viceroy yielded, despite the protests of the Spanish merchants, and opened the port to non-Spanish shipping.

In May 1810 news arrived in Buenos Aires of the complete collapse of the Central Junta and most of the legitimist forces in Spain. Pressured by the militia, the cabildo summoned a general meeting of leading local figures (following an ancient formula for times of crisis) called a *cabildo abierto,* or "open cabildo." While a mob, incited by political activists, vociferously demonstrated outside the hall, the cabildo abierto decided to depose the viceroy, now without claim to a mandate, and to organize their own ruling committee, or junta, to govern on behalf of the captured Ferdinand VII. One of the earliest acts of the junta was to remove all restraints upon European trade. It also exiled Spaniards who opposed the junta's policies, persecuted

Spanish merchants, and executed the Spanish leader of a counterrevolution—all in the name of Ferdinand VII, the rightful king of Spain.

Although ready to unite behind the issue of trade, the leaders in the junta were deeply divided on most other issues; these divergencies began to emerge at once. The leader of the junta was Cornelio Saavedra, a conservative leader of the urban militia who opposed efforts to transform the ideological and sociological foundations of the established order; but he was outnumbered by Mariano Moreno (who as editor of the official newspaper published a translation of Rousseau's *Social Contract*), Manuel Belgrano, and Bernardino Rivadavia, all of them liberals who wished not only to break ties with the makeshift Spanish regency but to institute reforms such as weakening the relationship between Church and state and establishing secular schools and a free press. Opposed to such steps, Saavedra resorted to the expedient of seating on the junta delegates from the interior cities, most of whom, of course, were conservative. The enlarged junta forced the resignation of Moreno after seven months in office—he died of natural causes shortly thereafter—and conveniently dispatched Belgrano to enforce the hegemony of Buenos Aires over Paraguay, a task for which he was unsuited by both temperament and training. Another liberal member of the junta undertook to extend its power over Bolivia and its silver mines, but loyalist forces based in highland Peru repulsed him.

The new and enlarged junta, rid of most of its more liberal members, lost much of its political support within Buenos Aires and proved to be too cumbersome for effective action. In September 1811 it named an executive triumvirate to rule with a rotating membership, but the resulting policies, not surprisingly, tended to be inconsistent. In the meantime the triumvirate's permanent secretary, the liberal Bernardino Rivadavia, accrued increasing influence. Under his direction steps were taken to put a final end to the slave trade, to encourage European immigration, and to end the system of special courts, or fueros. Rivadavia sought to link the region ever more closely to the world economy centered on England and to move toward a society made up of individuals, not corporations. The triumvirate was overthrown in late 1812 by a combination of dissident elements, some of whom felt Rivadavia had gone too far and others who believed he had not gone far enough. The succeeding triumvirate concentrated its attention on dealing with the centrifugal forces set loose by the break with Spain: If the Spanish Regency had no authority over the Río de la Plata, why should one city, Buenos Aires, rule over the rest? A congress was summoned in early 1813, but it immediately split into two groups, one made up of centralists, who were predominantly reformers, and the other consisting of provincial representatives, many of whom were more conservative. It never wrote a constitution, but did issue several laws. By using legal technicalities, liberals prevented some representatives from being seated, thus managing to form a majority which quickly proceeded to abolish the Inquisition, terminate titles of nobility, discard the practice of entailment, and declare that henceforth all children born of slave mothers were free. At the beginning of 1815, the congress appointed a young liberal, Carlos de Alvear, as chief executive, labeled supreme director; however, the congress still avoided a declaration of independence, precisely to skirt the divisive issue of centralism versus federalism as well as any decision on whether there should be a monarchy or a republic.

Meanwhile the Creole militia had been transformed into a regular army, filled by draftees and often officered by men who had served in the Spanish forces either in the colony or in Spain. It absorbed the bulk of public revenues, which came principally from the wealthy; some historians have argued that its formation represented a de facto redistribution of wealth to the seven thousand or so soldiers drawn from the artisanal and lower classes. Social change had begun.

The erratic and arbitrary actions of the self-seeking Alvear coupled with his liberalism-cum-centralism led to his overthrow by discontents who relied upon the power of the Uruguayan caudillo, José Gervasio Artigas (1764–1850), for support. By this time Artigas, fiercely committed to autonomy from direct control by either Spain or Buenos Aires, headed a loose confederation of five hostile provinces to the north of Buenos Aires. These provinces wanted as direct an access to foreign trade as that enjoyed by Buenos Aires. On the other hand, the western and northwestern provinces suffered an economic decline provoked by the opening of the port of Buenos Aires to the trade of all nations and the end of the Spanish monopoly system. Now their wine, their sugar, and their textiles had to compete with imports from Europe or Brazil. Two of them (Córdoba and Santa Fe) went so far as to declare their outright independence from Buenos Aires without resolving whether or not they were independent of Spain. This step enabled them to set up their own customhouses to control trade. As well, these provinces were alarmed at the liberal measures decreed in Buenos Aires. Finally, conservative groups in Buenos Aires now appealed to the interior provinces for political support against the liberals and summoned another constituent congress to meet not in Buenos Aires but in the interior city of Tucumán. It met in May 1816, and its actions form part of another chapter in the independence movement. By that date only Argentina and Paraguay were free of peninsular control.

Uruguay

When news arrived in Montevideo of the usurpation of the Spanish throne in 1808, the leaders of Montevideo immediately began to quarrel with those of Buenos Aires. They accused Viceroy Liniers, who had been chosen by the leaders of Buenos Aires, of being pro-French, a traitor to the Spanish crown, and therefore unworthy of their loyalty. They formed their own junta with the Spanish governor in Montevideo at the head. These actions were not entirely surprising since Montevideo had been primarily a fortified city with a large Spanish garrison. The junta voluntarily disbanded itself when Spain sent out a replacement for Liniers. But in 1810, when the junta of Buenos Aires, which claimed to govern on behalf of Ferdinand VII, replaced that viceroy and asked for the adherence of Montevideo, the latter refused, declaring its loyalty to the Spanish regency, which, after all, also ruled in the name of the king. The regency then named another viceroy for the region and made Montevideo the viceregal capital instead of Buenos Aires. Thus, Uruguayan independence from Buenos Aires overshadowed independence from Spain.

When Spanish officials began to use Montevideo as a base of operations against the new government in Buenos Aires, however, many Creoles in Montevideo became uneasy. Furthermore, Artigas, the leader of the Uruguayan gauchos, defected to the side of Buenos Aires and began a lightning campaign against the Spaniards in Montevideo, which reduced the area under Spanish control to the limits of the city itself. The Spanish viceroy appealed for help to the Portuguese monarch in Rio de Janeiro, whose wife, the sister of Ferdinand VII, claimed to be the rightful ruler of Spain in his absence. The Portuguese sent in an army. Faced with the Spanish forces in Montevideo and the slowly advancing Portuguese army in the interior of Uruguay, the Buenos Aires government signed a truce in late 1811 agreeing to let the Spanish viceroy control all of Uruguay. The Portuguese retreated under British pressure. Inconsolable, Artigas and four-fifths of the population of the hinterland of Uruguay retreated to the Argentine province of Entre Ríos, where they remained for more than a year before regrouping and returning to continue the fight against the Spaniards.

Meanwhile, Artigas' relations with Buenos Aires deteriorated. He sent delegates to the congress called by the liberals in 1813 and there demanded a federative government with local autonomy for the provinces. Since this congress failed to grant him what he wanted— indeed, failed to seat his delegates—he turned against it and fought both the Spaniards and the *porteños* (residents of Buenos Aires) simultaneously.

When the restoration of Ferdinand VII in 1814 appeared imminent, the government in Buenos Aires became desperate to rid the Río de la Plata region of Spanish rule. Montevideo served as a lodestone for Spanish forces invading from Bolivia and could also be used as a beachhead for armies dispatched from Spain. The government in Buenos Aires enlisted the support of William Brown, an Irishman, who, commanding a makeshift fleet, blockaded Montevideo from the sea. The residents of Montevideo actively aided the Spanish in their efforts to defeat the porteños; nevertheless, in June 1814 the city surrendered, and Buenos Aires again controlled it. But then Buenos Aires once again attempted an unsuccessful domination of Uruguay and Artigas recaptured Montevideo in early 1815.

Artigas instituted as enlightened a government as could be expected in such years of crisis, while he expanded his power in northeastern Argentina. Among other things he declared that the lands and cattle confiscated from wealthy European Spaniards and his other enemies would be distributed in small plots to the poor, regardless of race or other impediment. These land grants, had he stayed in power long enough to make them, would have been made inalienable to prevent the greedy from buying them up and reconstituting large estates. He also decreed the freedom of all slaves. These measures alarmed his fellow ranchers and property owners, but before they could oppose him he faced the even more threatening return of a Portuguese army.

Paraguay

Buenos Aires had even less success in imposing its old hegemony over Paraguay than over Uruguay. A relatively poor area from which the principal exports had been *yerba maté* (a leaf used in making tea throughout southern South America) and some tobacco and where settlements still faced the constant danger of Indian attacks, Paraguay had remained relatively isolated throughout the colonial period, developing strong sentiments of local loyalty. Its hacendados managed the work of a dependent workforce of mestizos and settled Guaraní Indians. In the capital city of Asunción men born in Spain controlled commerce and dominated the cabildo, not to mention the post of intendant. By the early nineteenth century the Creoles and those mestizos rich enough to pass as Creoles resented not only the Spaniards' predominance in Asunción but also the fact that Paraguay's exports had to pass through fiscal bottlenecks in Buenos Aires to reach their markets.

When news arrived of the events in Buenos Aires of May 1810, a cabildo abierto in Asunción quickly repudiated the claims to authority put forward by the porteños and promised its allegiance to the regency in Spain. When faced with a military incursion of seven hundred men from Buenos Aires led by Belgrano, the Paraguayans quickly mobilized five thousand militiamen and easily crushed the invaders.

The hacendados naturally controlled the Paraguayan countryside; in the city they now found an ally in Gaspar Rodríguez de Francia, a Creole lawyer who sat on the cabildo. Trained in theology at the University of Córdoba, he had an authoritarian streak in his character and a taciturn and secretive personality. In May 1811 the Creoles deposed the Spanish intendant and formally (and definitively) declared their independence from Spain, stating that they would cooperate with Buenos Aires only as equals. Francia sat on the junta set up at that time, but he frequently absented himself to travel in the interior, soliciting support from small landowners and Guaraní-speaking peasants. When an elected congress convened in 1813, he had little difficulty in persuading it to name him one of its two "consuls," and, when still another congress gathered in 1814, it made him Supreme Dictator. Counting always on the support of the poorer masses, he ruled the country until 1840.

Meanwhile, the big issue was to secure free navigation of the Paraná River. If Buenos Aires could not impose its will on the inland country, it could at least control its access to the sea. Based on its claims to sovereignty over Paraguay, Buenos Aires sometimes blocked all shipping in or out and always taxed it. It imposed an embargo on exports of Paraguayan tobacco and began buying its maté from Brazil. Meanwhile, the caudillos who arose on either side of the river in Argentina seized arms destined for Paraguay and raided river traffic without fear of punishment. Eventually Francia determined to go it alone, turning the economy and the culture inward, insisting on self-sufficiency, and rebuffing all foreigners. Public lands were turned into state enterprises for the production of livestock and foodstuffs, and small manufacturing enterprises made substitutes for imported goods. Aside from some trade with Brazil, Paraguay opted out of the international economy.

Chile

At the time of Napoleon's usurpation of the Spanish throne an interim governor ruled Chile. Events in Europe encouraged the Creole intellectuals who desired independence to speak out against his ineptitude, which brought upon them his uncontrolled and intemperate wrath. The governor's overreaction only widened the intellectuals' circle of adherents among the Creole aristocracy, who already distrusted the local Spaniards' true loyalty to the deposed king. Of course, the Spaniards in turn suspected the Creole aristocracy of lacking loyalty to Spain and accused them of wishing to rule themselves in the guise of loyalty to Ferdinand VII. When the governor heard that the Central Junta in Seville had collapsed and that a junta had been formed in Buenos Aires, he moved with special severity against three leading Creoles of Santiago, banishing them to Peru. This action resulted in open protests, for he had overreached himself. The audiencia itself forced his resignation in July 1810.

The next man in line for the governorship was in his dotage, but the audiencia supported him, hoping that his Chilean birth would satisfy the Creoles and that his age would make him easy to manipulate. The Creoles, however, were more adept at using him than were the Spaniards, and he agreed to summon a cabildo abierto. The Spaniards did not appear, either because they were not allowed by the Creole militia to enter the hall or, more probably, because they did not wish to undergo the humiliation of being outvoted at such a gathering. The cabildo abierto accepted the resignation of the new governor and named a junta to rule instead, still on behalf of the king.

The junta sought to win political favor by instituting some reforms, dissolving the audiencia, convoking a national assembly, and opening trade to all nations, thus breaking the formal ties to the exclusive commercial system of the empire. Moderate and conservative Creoles controlled the national assembly which convened in July 1811, and they wished to limit their actions to a few further reforms, to send delegates to the Spanish Cortes, and to stop short of any radical alterations in the status quo. But another group in the assembly, smaller but more liberal, wanted to declare independence and establish a republic.

One of these liberal leaders in the national assembly was Bernardo O'Higgins (1778–1842), the illegitimate son of an Irish-born intendant in Concepción who had later become viceroy of Peru. O'Higgins was partially educated in England, where he met Francisco de Miranda and acquired many liberal ideas. When his father died, he inherited considerable properties in southern Chile and returned there in 1802, a man of substance but with seditious views.

Alongside O'Higgins in spirit, although not a member of the national assembly, was the lawyer Juan Martínez de Rozas (1759–1813). He had once been a legal adviser for O'Higgins' father and had subsequently held various positions of authority, but his Creole origin had frustrated his desire for preferment beyond a certain level.

Another liberal leader in the national assembly was the political economist Manuel de Salas (1755–1841). He was more interested in increased autonomy than in outright independence; his opinions carried much weight.

When the national assembly named an executive committee to rule while a constitution was being drawn up, not one of the liberals was included. They resigned from the assembly in protest. Their resignation stirred to action the three Carrera brothers, Luís, Juan, and José, sons of one of the wealthiest and most influential Creole families in Chile. Luís, Juan, and their father had been active in the protests against the governor; José had been in Spain at the time as an officer in the Spanish army. Upon his return to Chile, José became fully committed to independence. He was dismayed by the moderate tenor of the national assembly and by the predominance in it of a rival wealthy Creole family. When the liberal members resigned, he determined on more forceful action. Winning over elements of the Creole militia, he led a coup d'état which purged the national assembly of the more conservative leaders and introduced a majority of liberals.

The new national assembly immediately proceeded to transform the old institutions. It abolished the Inquisition, created a single national court system, set up a new educational network, and declared free the children born of slaves. By interfering in the system of parochial fees, putting parish priests on a fixed salary, and creating secular cemeteries, it began the long struggle between Church and state which characterized the next century of Chilean history. This national assembly was short-lived, and many of its reforms were quickly undone, but it accomplished the task of spelling out in practical measures the implications of the Enlightenment.

José Carrera soon decided that, if one coup d'état had worked so well, two would be better; he dissolved the assembly and created a triumvirate with himself at the head and O'Higgins as another member. Tiring of this arrangement, he led still a third coup d'état and placed himself in sole command. He introduced a series of reforms, among them setting up the first printing press, decreeing the establishment of primary schools in every town, and combining three Church seminaries of Santiago into the secular National Institute.

But other liberals were offended by Carrera's arbitrary methods and by the aspects of a family feud which he had introduced into the struggle. Civil war broke out between the forces he led and those commanded by O'Higgins and Martínez de Rozas. The regionalism so characteristic of Spanish Americans also came into play since both of these men were from the southern province of Concepción and opposed efforts by Carrera to rule the entire country from Santiago.

These petty quarrels laid the groundwork for a larger crisis. The viceroy in Peru dispatched a Spanish force by sea to southern Chile, and, marching northward from there, it met Carrera's forces at Concepción, which fell in March 1813. Carrera's alleged mismanagement of the campaign brought about his deposition and temporary replacement by O'Higgins. O'Higgins moved to strike a truce with the Spaniards, for he preferred a pro forma declaration of loyalty to Spain and the election of representatives to the Spanish Cortes to continued bloody military encounters. Carrera, however, was outraged and led his fourth successful coup d'état. Although their quarrel was momentarily patched up, Carrera's rancor led him at a crucial moment to refuse reinforcements to O'Higgins, who with his army was forced to flee over the Andes to Argentina, where he joined the army of General José de San Martín. The Spanish army proceeded to conquer and was in control of Santiago by October 1814. A brutal repression followed, and Spanish monopoly merchants found their privileges restored. A new cabildo was formed, made up almost entirely of guild merchants.

Venezuela

Venezuela was the first Spanish colony to be informed of the usurpation of the Spanish throne in 1808. A French agent was sent to Caracas to demand the allegiance of the colony. He was met with a cold reception from the captain general and a hostile mob commanded by Creole militia officers. However, when the officers requested permission from the captain-general to form a local junta as in Spain, he temporarily threw them into jail for their audacity. Later, when news arrived of the final collapse of the Central Junta of Seville, the officers initiated their plan without the cooperation of the captain general (whom they deposed in April 1810), formed a junta, and immediately worked to establish its power. The junta deported the captain-general and the members of the audiencia, successfully solicited the support of most of the other cities in the region, opened the ports to world trade, granted preferential tariffs to the British, and dispatched diplomatic missions to London and Washington to seek at least tacit support. Simón Bolívar was one of the diplomats sent to London, and there he recruited on his own initiative the support of Francisco de Miranda, who returned to Caracas with him. Bolívar and Miranda elaborated an ideology and pressed the congress, which 'the junta finally convened in March 1811, to declare independence. The American Confederation of Venezuela was created on July 7, 1811.

The act of declaring independence proved unfortunate. The revolutionaries, scions of the landowners and educated in a European intellectual milieu, in their desire for independence did not know how far they had outdistanced the majority of the population, even many in their own class; they also forgot how near Venezuela was to the

Spanish strongholds in the Caribbean. Many Venezuelans who would have been placated by a declaration of loyalty to the absent king considered a declaration of independence as equivalent to cursing God. Under the current social order, this act was suicidal. Those who would have supported the idea of a junta modeled on the one in Seville were puzzled or dismayed. The pardos were distressed, for the Creoles, who had oppressed them the most, were now in control; a property qualification for voting made it very clear that this movement was not theirs. The Spanish officials and clergy, who had been more solicitous of pardo welfare and had often ignored the silly prejudices of the Creoles, were out of power. Slavery was maintained, provoking a series of slave revolts. The Spanish, therefore, found it easy to enlist the support of the pardos, while desertions plagued the revolutionary army, by necessity made up of pardo draftees and slaves marshaled by landowners.

The Spanish garrison from Puerto Rico, which landed in the loyal northwestern part of Venezuela in 1812, had little trouble in gathering support and advancing rapidly toward Caracas. Despite the hurried elevation of Miranda to generalissimo and virtual dictator, nothing could stem the advancing Spanish loyalist tide. Miranda capitulated and tried to escape with the treasury, presumably to fight again as he had done before, but Bolívar, who had once idolized Miranda, put another interpretation on this act and turned him over to the victorious Spanish in exchange for a safe-conduct for himself to Colombia.[1] There he pondered his past experiences and planned for the future.

Simón Bolívar (1783–1830) emerged as the great hero of Spanish-American independence. A native of Caracas, he was the son of a wealthy Creole who owned two cacao plantations, three cattle ranches, a very large number of slaves, and thirteen houses. He received his earliest education through a well-read tutor who was so thoroughly impregnated with the ideas of Rousseau that he made

---

[1] The name Colombia was first coined by Bolívar for a country he created from parts of the Viceroyalty of New Granada, a country which included approximately what is today Venezuela, Ecuador, Colombia, and Panamá. By 1830 it had dissolved into its constituent segments as we know them today (except for Panamá), although Colombia itself was known as New Granada until 1863. We shall use the name "Colombia" in its present sense and refer, as do other historians, to Bolívar's chimerical creation as Gran Colombia.

Simón Bolívar, Liberator of
Northern South America

Émile his guide for the boy's instruction. Bolívar became a strong
admirer of Enlightenment thinkers even before he went to Spain in
1799 to complete his education. In Europe Bolívar traveled widely
and lived in Paris when Napoleon was in his glory. He moved freely
within high society, enjoyed Parisian pleasures, and studied Napoleon's military tactics. He later copied many of them in his own
campaigns. Bolívar returned to Caracas and joined the Creole militia
officers who expressed political discontent in 1810.

Colombia was in political turmoil when Bolívar arrived there. He
tried to persuade the new insurgent government that it would not be
safe from Spanish authority until Venezuela had been freed. The
government refused to heed his warning; Bolívar disobeyed its orders
and led a successful campaign against the Spaniards in eastern Venezuela. When he returned bearing treasure, he was not court-martialed
but promoted to general.

Bolívar continued to dream of returning to Caracas in glory. After
much pleading, the insurgent government in Colombia gave him five
hundred men to undertake an expedition in 1813. He moved eastward
with lightning speed, repeatedly engaging the Spaniards before they
realized he was near, and occupied Caracas within three months. His
campaign was a procession of triumphs against great odds, unparal-
leled since the days of the conquistadors; it was also a great learning

experience for him. During the campaign he perfected his ability to command and experimented with propaganda. He virtually created the public manifesto, now so traditional in Latin America. He also developed the triumphal entry to win over the masses: His great carriage was drawn through flower-strewn streets by dozens of pretty young women; the crowds went wild with adulation.

Bolívar's campaign had by no means completely crushed the Spaniards in Venezuela. They clearly perceived the divisions in Venezuelan society and now managed to enlist the full support of the llaneros, who were ready to fight against the hated city types and the haughty Creoles. To mobilize the llaneros the Spaniards turned to José Tomás Boves. Boves was a sadistic Spanish adventurer who had been arrested for smuggling by the Creole government. The Spaniards released him when they took over in 1812, and he immediately offered his services to them in exchange for booty. Boves had long been familiar with the ways of the llaneros, and, by being as hard as they, he had won their respect. Eventually ten thousand llaneros, almost all on horseback, were at his command. Incensed by earlier republican measures that threatened to end the open range to the benefit of would-be ranchers among the Creoles, they also fought for the booty Boves distributed among them. In addition, Boves obtained the special loyalty of blacks and pardos by promoting them over the lighter-skinned officers in his command.

Bolívar was no sooner in possession of Caracas in 1813 than Boves loosed his hordes against him. Striking more swiftly than Bolívar and outdoing him in forcefulness, Boves was soon successful. Bolívar's troops began to melt away. By mid-1814 Bolívar was once more in flight; the class divisions of Venezuela had defeated him.

Colombia

There was relatively little reaction in Colombia to the 1808 usurpation of the Spanish throne. The legitimacy of the viceroy was not in question since he had been appointed by the king. He accepted the authority of the Central Junta of Seville and had relatively little difficulty in quelling an abortive revolt in Quito the following year. But, when news arrived of the collapse of the Central Junta, the viceroy's power began to wane. The cabildo of the coastal city of

Cartagena petitioned and secured from the local governor the right to participate in his decisions and to open the port to trade of all nations. The leading citizens of Bogotá demanded that the viceroy summon a cabildo abierto. He was forced to comply when the Creole militia defected from his camp. Inspired by the lawyer Camilo Torres (1766–1816), the cabildo abierto organized a supreme junta in July 1810. The junta declared loyalty to Ferdinand VII but would not surrender its right to govern unless he came to rule them in person. Meanwhile, it summoned a constitutional convention with representatives from all provinces and instructed it to create a charter to include a federal system in which provincial autonomy would be protected.

Jealousies immediately arose between Bogotá and the other Colombian cities, with Cartagena spearheading the opposition. The next year the supreme junta in Bogotá, admitting reality, called a local congress to draft a constitution just for the surrounding province of Cundinamarca. The junta also invited representatives from the other provinces to draft a pact between the acknowledged sovereign provinces. The representatives met, formed a congress, and in November 1811 established a very loose confederation, the United Provinces of New Granada, but it made no formal declaration of independence.

Some in Bogotá, however, were unwilling to make concessions to the regionalist feeling; among them was Antonio Nariño, who had emerged from house arrest in 1810. He insisted that unity was essential if Colombia was to withstand the onslaught of Spanish power and demanded that Colombia form a strong central government. When his preachments fell on deaf ears, he decided on more forceful action. Leading a coup d'état in Bogotá, he tore up the provincial constitution and proceeded to conquer neighboring provinces. Many of his officers resigned in protest and joined the forces of the beleaguered victims. Nariño meanwhile assumed increasingly dictatorial powers in the province of Cundinamarca and became steadily more unbalanced. Under his frantic leadership Cundinamarca seceded from the United Provinces of New Granada in the name of centralism.

The Spaniards took advantage of this internal political turmoil and mounted an offensive against the insurgents, until Nariño and the United Provinces finally agreed to cooperate with each other militarily. But it was too late. The war went badly; Nariño was captured in 1814, the local royalists in the northern city of Santa Marta revolted and reestablished Spanish control there, and the provinces began to fight among themselves once again. Then the congress of the United Provinces decided that the province of Cundinamarca must be forced to join the union. At this moment Bolívar returned from Venezuela after his second defeat and was given this task. He occupied Bogotá at the end of 1814. He next turned his attention to driving the Spanish out of the north, only to discover that Cartagena would not cooperate, partly for fear of losing its hoard of military stores and partly because of personal jealousies. Disgusted, he left Colombia and retired to Jamaica. In May 1816 Bogotá fell, and by August all of Colombia was back in Spanish hands.

The leaders of the movement had invariably been drawn from the upper classes of Colombia. Fortunately for them, social tensions had not surfaced. The elites, however, managed to undo their revolution all by themselves, and the Spanish forces had an easy time of it.

Ecuador, Peru, and Bolivia

The rest of Spanish South America hardly felt the First War of Independence. Reform-minded Creole intellectuals established abortive juntas in La Paz, Bolivia, and Quito, Ecuador, as early as 1809 and later hatched unsuccessful plots in Lima, Peru. When delegates selected by Peruvian cabildos in 1810 arrived at the Spanish Cortes in Cádiz they argued against establishing a broad suffrage, even though this would have increased the weight of American delegations to future cortes. Their reason? It would have enfranchised Indians and mestizos, whose political weight they feared. Not surprisingly, Creole militias from Lima later fought on the side of the Spanish against the insurgents in Chile and Bolivia. In 1814 Creoles and mestizos in Cuzco rose against the European Spaniards, appealing to Indian chiefs for support. But when they got it, they were appalled at what their folly had wrought: Indian masses, oriented by a messianic vision, ransacked cities, killed whites indiscriminately, and destroyed much property. Most of the Creoles fell away as a Spanish army brought the Indians down with great cruelty.

Invading revolutionary armies, recruited in Argentina, momentarily liberated southern Bolivia, but these initial victories were deceptive. What the bulk of the population—made up of Indians—wanted, the revolutionaries could promise but not give them: time to tend their own crops on village lands and freedom from labor obligations in the mines. The plainsmen from Argentina were soon driven off. Argentine armies made two more attempts, one led by Belgrano, to conquer this mountainous region; both failed. These areas of traditionalism felt no interest in the ideas of the Enlightenment and stood to gain nothing from closer contacts with northern Europe. On the whole, social tensions led the Creole elites to side with the Spanish. Aside from some sporadic guerrilla activity among poorer whites and mestizos, the First War of Independence passed this region by.

Mexico

When news arrived in Mexico of the abdication of Charles IV in 1808, José de Iturrigaray, the viceroy appointed by the corrupt Spanish minister Godoy, feared that he would be stripped of his lucrative position, for the Spanish community in Mexico City not only despised him as an unworthy representative of the mother country but also suspected him of siding with the French as Godoy had. In the hope of securing his position, Iturrigaray summoned a joint meeting of the audiencia and cabildo; no consensus emerged, for cabildo members argued that according to sixteenth-century authorities sovereignty reverted to the people in the absence of the king and that the cabildos represented the people, while the erudite judges of the audiencia would hear none of it. Iturrigaray finally sided with the cabildo, agreed with it to form a local junta, and consented to head it, apparently believing that this would make him personally more secure than if he obeyed the junta in Spain. Satisfied with his cleverness, he proceeded to rule as if nothing had happened. The Creoles were momentarily satisfied. But Spanish monopoly merchants were outraged and successfully carried out a plot to seize Iturrigaray. They especially feared that a more representative body would be summoned to replace the junta and that the voice of the castas would then be heard. The audiencia, privy to the plot from the beginning, met at two o'clock in the morning and named a new viceroy. The Spaniards were in control again. The attempt at revolution from above thus ended ignominiously, but, by overthrowing the viceroy, the conservatives had done much to undermine the very legitimacy of the Spanish rule they intended to uphold.

Despite the insurrectionary ferment spreading among the Creoles, little else happened in almost two years to suggest the momentous events that were next to overtake Mexico. In 1810 a new and able viceroy arrived: Francisco Xavier Venegas, who was closely associated with the monopoly merchants of Spain. But as developments in Spain moved toward the defeat of the patriot forces there, secret societies and clandestine meetings of dissident Creoles became increasingly common in Mexico. One group of conspirators, meeting in Querétaro, planned a coup d'état for December 1810 in which the Creole militia would play a central role; but in their efforts to secure support, they approached some who betrayed the plot to the Spanish authorities. The plotters, warned of their imminent arrest, scattered and hid except for one: Miguel Hidalgo.

HIDALGO   Miguel Hidalgo y Costilla (1753–1811) was a parish priest. Not particularly devout or parsimonious—in fact, he was rather profligate—Hidalgo had a good education, kept up with the ideas of the Enlightenment, and was deeply concerned with the plight of his parishioners, the Indians around Dolores. He had been banished there by the Inquisition because of his many peccadillos and dangerous ideas. The majority of his parishioners lived under subhuman conditions; a couple of bad harvests had pushed up the price of corn, and they had reached a breaking point. Although the production of grapes and the cultivation of mulberry trees for silkworms had been forbidden in America because of the competition such activity gave to the merchants in Spain, Hidalgo encouraged the Indians to undertake these ventures and also helped them establish a brickyard, pottery, and tannery. The companionship of unlettered Indians, however, was not enough to satisfy the roving curiosity of a well-read man who also enjoyed good living. He sought out like-minded fellows in nearby Querétaro and was brought into the conspiracy plot. Evidently he was not the driving force behind the plot, but when the others fled, he decided to carry out a modified plan on his own.

At dawn on Sunday, September 16, 1810, Hidalgo summoned his flock to the parish church. Addressing them in their native tongue, he pointed out their miserable condition and blamed the Spaniards for it. He simultaneously declared his loyalty to captured Ferdinand VII, whom the Indians had been taught to venerate as an almost messianic figure, and accused the king's subordinates of being untrue to their master. "Down with the Spanish! Down with bad govern-ment!" The Indians scurried to assemble machetes, pikes, clubs, and axes and followed him to the next village, where a similar scene took place. "Long live the Blessed Virgin of Guadalupe!" became their cry as they appealed to the particularly Mexican, particularly Indian, madonna. Then to still another village marched the throng. Within a few days Hidalgo headed a crowd of several thousand, including some mestizos and a few Creole plotters who hastened out of hiding. An attempt to transform the inchoate mass into a disciplined force failed. Since supplies were scanty, they raided haciendas, consumed crops and cattle, and also drew away the workers as new recruits. Then the crowd tackled towns, plundering the shops, sacking the houses, raping the white women, and smashing the machinery of mines and craft shops. When they invaded Guanajuato, a mining town already racked by discord between mine workers and mine owners, the bloodshed was unrestrained and the destruction of property devas-tating. It was a war of revenge against centuries of oppression.

Although a few Creole intellectuals in Mexico City continued to defend Hidalgo, most people of substance and education considered him a madman. Hidalgo did little to stop the mob, for he understood

Miguel Hidalgo, Hero of
Mexican Independence

their frustration and sympathized with their outburst. When he realized the effect their destructive campaign had on others, however, he began to have doubts himself. And his Creole companions were appalled: They had hoped for a rebellion, not a social revolution.

Hidalgo next moved toward Mexico City, leading some eighty thousand men. After a bloody day-long battle, in which the Indians suffered enormous losses, they nevertheless succeeded in driving back the Spanish military contingent of twenty-five hundred soldiers sent out to defend the mountain passes surrounding the city. Then, on the brim of the valley, Hidalgo hesitated, changed his mind, and directed the mob to turn away from Mexico City.

The reasons for Hidalgo's decision are still disputed. Some historians claim that his sensitive soul recoiled at the thought of witnessing another scene of pillage and bloodshed. Others have suggested more practical reasons: The plan for an immediate rising of Creoles, stimulated by the initial victories won by the castas, might have worked if Hidalgo had been able to launch an effective propaganda campaign making clear his goals—if he had any—and appealing for the Creoles' support before the gory details about Guanajuato had reached their attention. But he lacked a printing press, and the royalists had several. They distributed thousands of handbills throughout the major cities describing the bloody ravages of Hidalgo's horde, and these accounts were spread further through sermons and by word of mouth. Neither people of property nor their urban employees could identify with such a movement. Even more significantly, the village Indians of the valley of Mexico, who were to have been more recruits for Hidalgo, turned against him. Finally, Hidalgo knew that a large Spanish army was descending on the city from the north. If he occupied the city, his followers would likely turn to looting and drinking and be easy prey for the advancing army.

This loyalist army had been drawn from two sources: the regular Spanish army, originally posted in the north and on the coast to withstand threats from French or English invaders (and into which so many locals had been forcibly drafted that they formed the vast majority of the soldiers), and the Creole militias. This latter category, despite some early exceptions as in Guanajuato itself, gradually turned against Hidalgo and ended up siding with the Spanish. Hastily brought together by the Spanish general Félix María Calleja, a peninsular military commander who had lived for many years in Mexico and was well related to the Creole elite, these men proved increasingly a well-disciplined and effective fighting force, all the more important since no reinforcements would come from Spain until 1812. Ironically, Calleja thus constructed a Mexican army, filled with Mexican troops and mostly commanded by Mexican officers; should it ever turn on Spain, it would be a formidable enemy. But for now they opposed the revolution.

When Hidalgo turned back from Mexico City, his movement lost its momentum. He fought one last major battle in early November 1810, in which desperate Indians tried to stop the Spanish cannons even with sombreros. The battle was lost when a magazine exploded and the resulting grass fire spread panic among Hidalgo's ranks. The Spanish soldiers moved in ruthlessly. Some adventurers fought on, but the first phase of the Mexican war for independence had ended. Hidalgo fled north to Querétaro and eventually was betrayed, tried, and executed on July 31, 1811. His head remained mounted on a stake in Guanajuato for ten years as a grisly reminder of the fate awaiting rebels. Hidalgo had settled nothing, but he is remembered as the first hero of Mexican independence.

The effort so far was more akin to the rebellion of Tupac Amaru in Peru than to the other struggles for independence in Spanish America. The long-pent-up hatreds of the Indians gave impetus to both movements, even though Hidalgo's followers were not, like those in Peru, village Indians with an ancient sedentary lineage. Well-educated leaders intent on reform rather than revolution and inspired at least partially by the new thought of the Enlightenment lit both sparks. Both leaders hesitated to invade major cities, the capture of which could have paved the way to final success. And in both cases the movements frightened men of property away from any thought of revolutionary solutions to their problems. But timing often gives a meaning to historical events which is not built into their logic. It was the thought of independence—or at least autonomy—that sparked the activity of Hidalgo, and this purpose was read into his movement by both friendly and hostile observers. This meaning was picked up and borne further by his immediate successors. The social significance of the movement, as opposed to the political message, only affected the effort adversely and was not hailed for at least another generation.

With Hidalgo gone, and even as he lived, other leaders sprang up in various parts of Mexico. Many of them had originally been commissioned by Hidalgo to spread the revolution into their districts. The Spanish general Calleja noted that "the insurrection . . . returns like the hydra, in proportion to the number of times its head is cut off."[2] Often parish priests or members of the lower middle class such as muleteers or shopkeepers took up the cause. Some chiefs were no more than brigands, while others specifically sought the redress of their fellows' local grievances. Just south of Guadalajara, for example, two Indians—Encarnación Rosas and José de Santa Anna—found widespread support among villagers who had been harshly treated by the vengeful Spaniards in the wake of Hidalgo's defeat. Their redoubt was an island in Lake Chapala on which a prison had once stood; still fortified, it proved almost impregnable. Some thousand men armed with fourteen cannons and three hundred muskets held off the Spanish enemy. In mid-1813 loyalist forces attacked with nine boats carrying six hundred men and four twenty-four-pound mortars. And still the Indians repulsed them. Attempts to lay siege to the island proved equally unsuccessful despite the assignment of eight thousand soldiers to the effort, because the villages surrounding the lake managed to keep the insurgent garrison supplied for over three long years. During that time the insurgents regularly stole ashore and engaged the Spanish in guerrilla warfare, often in concert with other insurgent groups, who communicated with them by using smoke signals. Finally the Spanish commander offered a truce, including a general amnesty for all participants and promises to rebuild the villages, restock their herds, supply seeds for the next planting season, and make José de Santa Anna the legitimate "governor" of the island fortress. Only then did peace return to the region. Meanwhile, to the south, a much more important offshoot of Hidalgo's revolt had seriously threatened to end Spanish rule in Mexico altogether.

MORELOS   One of Hidalgo's lieutenants who continued to fight was José Maria Morelos (1765–1815). Morelos, a mestizo trying to rise within the lower middle class, had quit his work as a muleteer on the Mexico City–Acapulco route to enter a seminary and study for the priesthood. The rector of the seminary at that time had been

---

[2] Quoted by Timothy E. Anna, *The Fall of the Royal Government in Mexico* (Lincoln, Neb.: University of Nebraska Press, 1978), p. 85.

Hidalgo, for this was before he had been banished to Dolores. Upon completion of his studies, Morelos was named priest for a parish in the hot, humid valley of the Balsas River. When he heard about Hidalgo's mad adventure, he rushed to join his ex-teacher, who told him to return to the Balsas River valley and foster revolution there.

In this task Morelos proved more successful than his mentor because he was a skillful organizer as well as a man of perseverance. Depending on peasants who could be fierce fighters one moment and peaceful tillers of the soil the next, he proceeded to conduct a large-scale guerrilla war that intimidated the Creole landowners and destroyed the system of Spanish control in the southern regions of Mexico. He also welded disparate interests into one cause. He soon attracted financial and moral support from those, including local potentates, who wished to be on the winning side. With Creoles he pushed national pride and doctrines of popular sovereignty. Yet he also advocated complete racial equality, the abolition of the fueros, and the end of the corporate society. Going even further, he decreed the breaking up of the large estates into smallholdings, the abolition of the tribute, the seizure of Church lands, and other radical reforms designed to bind the loyalty of the masses. He nevertheless struggled successfully to keep his movement from becoming a race war; it would be a nationalist effort above all else.

By the beginning of 1813 he had gathered an army of nine thousand men. It probably included more mestizos than Indians, but Indians from communal villages that Hidalgo had failed to mobilize often joined Morelos' ranks. Still, he found it difficult to attract hacienda peons if their masters had played the patriarchal role and supplied the workers with rations, housing, and security. In many cases those who joined Morelos' cause did so to settle long-standing local grievances, not to carry forward a national project. To arm his troops he relied on captured Spanish weapons, and they rode on stolen horses. He had taken the rich city of Oaxaca (in November 1812) and controlled all of Mexico south of Mexico City, Puebla, and Veracruz, except Acapulco; he was able at times to completely cut the capital city off from its food-supplying regions.

Morelos used his power and influence to convene a congress of eight members to draft a constitution. Meeting in Chilpancingo, the congress first declared Mexico independent in November 1813. It then concentrated its attention on legal questions that perhaps should have been postponed. Bickering inevitably resulted. By the time they completed the constitution the next year, Morelos had lost most of the territory once under his command.

Morelos' biggest mistake was that he did not move on the capital when he could have done so. By the beginning of 1813, when he was at the height of his power, he was in contact with an active fifth column within Mexico City, which a contemporary Spaniard described as being made up of "shopkeepers, barbers, tailors, . . . that is to say, of low and common folk."[3] They were joined by some lawyers, government employees, and other professional men, who, having decided to pay more attention to Morelos' commitment to independence than to his social reforms, organized an effective intelligence and propaganda organization. The viceroy reported in desperation that they informed the revolutionaries on "the status of the forces, munitions, and supplies, all of which [information] is taken from the offices of the government; accounts of the resources of the government, its scarcities and its difficulties."[4] This group urged Morelos to move on Mexico City, assuring him that his name was now a byword and would enlist immediate support. But he failed to follow their advice. Instead, he spent the entire summer besieging the fortress city of Acapulco—apparently in a quixotic determination to carry out instructions received from Hidalgo three years earlier—while the Spanish army smashed the strongholds of his allies and left him isolated. The government then undertook a vigorous counterinsurgency program in the south: It provided all propertied Creoles with arms on the gamble that they would not be used against the government. By the end of 1813 Morelos began to suffer major defeats, which continued for the next two years. Finally, the Spaniards encircled his last position and overran his fortifications. He was executed on December 22, 1815.

With Morelos gone (and Ferdinand VII returned to his throne), the independence movement lost its vigor. The Creole elite had never joined the revolutionary movement. Spanish forces consistently

---

[3] Quoted by David A. Brading, *Miners and Merchants in Bourbon Mexico, 1763–1810* (Cambridge, Eng.: Cambridge University Press, 1971), p. 346.

[4] Quoted by Wilbert H. Timmons, *Morelos: Priest, Soldier, Statesman of Mexico* (El Paso: Texas Western College Press, 1963), p. 86.

searched out and emptied the pockets of rebellion. Those whose loyalty to Spain was in doubt were at first persecuted and severely punished; later they received an amnesty. Many revolutionary leaders were either captured and executed or retired to private life, accepting pardons or disguising their identity. Others fought among themselves. A few bandits still remained at large, cloaking their activity with the banner of independence, but only two men of genuine patriotism continued in rebellion. Holed up in the hills, virtually hermits, Vicente Guerrero in the west and Felix Fernandez, alias Guadalupe Victoria, in the east, still dreamt of independence for Mexico.

Through them Morelos' memory lived on, for he had given the movement definition, institutionalized an independent government with its own constitution, and set forth a social agenda. Although his social reforms would first triumph decades—even a century—later, they reflected the steady pressure exerted on the system by the subaltern. Nevertheless, by the end of 1817 practically the entire country was at peace or at least ready to recognize that a stalemate had been reached. Perhaps 10 percent of Mexico's population had died during the wars, although many of them perished in an epidemic that raged during 1813, especially in the cities controlled by loyalist forces; Mexico City alone lost twenty thousand people, and seven thousand died in Puebla. It was a sad condition for the once prosperous colony.

Brazil

The complete independence of Brazil was secured gradually and almost imperceptibly over a period of twenty-three years beginning in 1808. During this time, events in Europe overtook Brazilians and impelled them along a course which they had hardly considered on their own. One may confidently maintain that in effect Brazil was independent by 1815, although Brazil celebrates 1822 as the date of independence, and in some other ways the process did not end until 1831.

The arrival of the Portuguese court and government in Rio de Janeiro in early 1808 transformed Brazil's status from an obscure colony to a seat of government. The new administration opened the ports to the trade of friendly nations—namely England—thus achieving for Brazil through a king's signature what the rest of Latin America had struggled for years to achieve. This measure legally marked the economic independence of Brazil. It was soon followed, however, by another kind of colonialism when the British insisted that the import duty of 24 percent be lowered to 15 percent for all goods from England. Dependent as John VI was on them for military support in driving the French out of Portugal, he had no recourse but to agree.

The new government fostered agricultural innovations, encouraged industries, established a national bank, and instituted a new judicial system (a step toward a single court system). The prince regent gave Rio de Janeiro a sophistication which it had hitherto not known because the splendor of viceroys had escaped it; it was now amply rewarded with the pomp and ceremony of a genuine European court. Furthermore, he directed the foundation of medical schools, a national museum, a national library, and a botanical garden. The royal press became Brazil's first printing establishment and in 1811 published Adam Smith's *Wealth of Nations*. Brazilian Creoles welcomed all these changes, but they also resented the interference of the newly arrived royal bureaucrats in matters they had heretofore managed on their own.

When Portugal was liberated from Napoleonic rule, the court was naturally expected to return, but John (crowned John VI in 1816 at the death of his mother) preferred to stay in Brazil. To solve this awkward problem, he elevated Brazil to the legal status of kingdom, making Rio de Janeiro its capital. As the king of two kingdoms he could reside in only one—and he chose Brazil. Thus by 1815 the country achieved a goal that Mexicans often dreamt of but never realized: bringing their king to rule among them. A revolution from above, tried so fleetingly and unsuccessfully in Mexico in 1808, succeeded easily in Brazil. Of course, the assumption of power by a viceroy cannot compare in significance with the arrival of a king and court, and, indeed, this disparity suggests that if the Spanish king had fled to Mexico, that nation's history might have been much more like Brazil's. There was no constitutional crisis in Brazil, so whatever dissatisfactions might have been present did not have occasion to surface.

* * *

Social revolution and political independence appear to have been antagonistic. In Mexico violent class warfare pointed the way toward social revolution, but it failed to produce political independence, indeed, hampered its emergence; whereas in Brazil social relationships remained virtually unchanged, but political independence was achieved without the use of force. One tentative conclusion to be derived from this juxtaposition is that it was precisely the crisis of legitimacy in Mexico that provided the opportunity for the emergence of social violence. If so, one would have to add that, although a necessary cause, such a political crisis was not a sufficient one to provoke social upheaval since in Venezuela the opposite resulted. In Mexico it was the Creoles' fear of social revolution that stymied political independence, whereas in Venezuela it was halted by the lower classes' fear of Creole dominance.

A comparison between Venezuela and Argentina reveals that, in spite of common interests in establishing closer ties with European markets and a shared infatuation with the ideas of the Enlightenment, these countries did not follow a common track. Venezuela was closer than Argentina to the Spanish military bases in the Caribbean and thus more easily subdued. The Venezuelan leaders, unlike the Argentine ones, made the error of declaring independence rather than insisting on their loyalty to the king; thus they alienated many who might have supported the more limited goal of a local junta ruling on behalf of the king. But, most important, the preexisting class hatred in Venezuela far exceeded the animosities between gauchos and urban residents in Argentina; and although friction between these groups in Argentina increased, no Spanish forces were in a position to take advantage of them as they had in Venezuela, mobilizing the llaneros.

A comparison between Argentina and Chile reveals several points at which their experiences resembled each other, but also significant differences. In both places Creole militia officers forced the formation of local juntas and the deposition of weak and demoralized Spanish administrators. Creole intellectuals—Moreno, Belgrano, and Rivadavia in Buenos Aires and O'Higgins, Martínez de Rozas, and Salas in Santiago—played a prominent role in the initial proceedings. In both areas, however, conservative forces arose to ease out the liberals. Since the liberals did not hesitate to use force to regain their earlier position, civil war ensued. Out of this chaos arose a new phenomenon: *caudillismo*, the appeal of the man on horseback, the man of deeds who establishes himself as dictator. Artigas on the east coast and the Carreras on the west exemplify it. Finally, in Chile the Spanish forces defeated the divided revolutionaries and reoccupied the country; whereas in Argentina it was they who were driven out despite the fractiousness of the Argentines. The limitations of Spanish military power and the relative locations of the two countries explains the result: Spanish armies in Peru could more easily reach Chile than Argentina.

In 1816 only the relatively isolated Argentina, Paraguay, and Uruguay were free of Spanish control. Elsewhere, regional rivalry, class hatreds, and divided leadership so weakened the revolutionary cause that by using small military contingents already in America in 1810 plus limited reinforcements from Europe after 1814, the Spanish succeeded, with the help of loyalist Creoles and revengeful lower-class elements, in crushing the revolutionary forces.

Outside Mexico, the most important result of the First War of Independence was the Creole experience of power. The Creole militias had been crucial agents of revolution in the first days. Indeed, how important they were is demonstrated by the exception: In Mexico they sided with the royalists and crushed the movement. Elsewhere the Creoles gained a sharpened awareness of the differences between their interests and those of the mother countries. Whenever and wherever they gained power, they exercised it to advance their distinct interests, especially to facilitate commerce with northern Europe. One of the first acts of practically every junta was to open the ports to British vessels.

Creole intellectuals also advanced some aspect of the Enlightenment worldview in all areas. In Chile and Argentina specific reform legislation was enacted. In Venezuela and Colombia the fighting, either with the Spanish or with other Creoles, was too intense to allow much time for the elaboration of a reform program. In Mexico the attempt to reform society alienated the very groups that might otherwise have cooperated in more modest goals. In Brazil the Portuguese government encouraged learning, scientific thought, and the notion that reason could lead Brazil toward economic development. Thus, although independence was not everywhere won, it was now recognized as a means toward larger goals and established as an ideal in a large part of Latin America.

Chapter Five
The Second War of Independence

There were two principal causes of the Second War of Independence. One was the First War of Independence and, in the case of Brazil, its experience of autonomy during the same period. Deep divisions between the former colonials and their mother countries resulted. The other cause was the restoration in many colonies of a harsh Spanish rule and the threat of such a restoration in Brazil. There could no longer be any doubt as to the difference of sentiment and goals between the Americans and the peninsulars. To explore the origins of this repressive tendency, we must first look to Europe.

Repercussion of European Events

Much as the First War had been provoked by developments outside America, just so did European events have a distinct effect on the course of the second one. With the defeat of Napoleon in 1814, a great conservative reaction swept across Europe. Years of revolution and warfare had left the people weary, and many sought a return to the old regime. Others were willing to accept some but not all of the changes in social organization wrought by the cataclysmic events of the previous quarter century. Elites everywhere worried that a resurgence of revolutionary fervor would further threaten their dominance and plunge Europe once again into war. Their fears were exacerbated by an economic depression that characterized the postwar years. Even in England habeas corpus was suspended, public meetings forbidden, and freedom of the press circumscribed. In France the restored Bourbon king issued a constitution that maintained a chamber of deputies, but ultraconservative legislators, who were in the majority, moved severely to restrict the freedom of the individual, while the courts were merciless in condemning former revolutionaries and Bonapartists. Several rulers of small German states granted their people constitutions, but none were drafted by elected bodies. Frederick William III of Prussia and Alexander I of Russia did not even do that much. Although Alexander at first dreamt romantically of instituting some sort of liberal regime built on Christian principles, he became steadily more conservative in the years after 1815. Prince Metternich, Europe's strongest advocate of dynastic legitimacy and social order, completely dominated Austria as prime minister. He also extended his influence over the Italian states, where, with his backing, rulers firmly squelched any effort toward individual liberty or popular sovereignty. Within this context, Spain's swing toward conservatism is not surprising.

When Ferdinand VII regained the throne of Spain after the Napoleonic invasion, there was much rejoicing both in Spain and in Spanish America. But the joy was short-lived. Ferdinand lacked any qualities of statesmanship or vision and he began by throwing out the Constitution of 1812, insisting on absolute power. He ignored all the liberal advances of previous years and even reversed reforms instituted by his grandfather, Charles III: He readmitted the Jesuits, restored the ancient rights of the nobility, and reinstituted the Inquisition. Although Ferdinand's conservative reaction garnered the support of the landed nobility, the morality of the court and the morale of the country remained as low as in the days of Godoy.

A number of factors contributed toward eventually weakening Ferdinand's rule. Since the king trusted no one who had ideas, only the most fawning adventurers rose at his court. The fabric of Spanish society had been frayed by years of civil war and the fierce hatreds it had engendered. Moreover, no longer did Spain receive rich revenues from the colonies; rather, as we shall see, the colonies represented a constant drain on state finances and Spanish manpower. The merchants who depended on monopoly trade saw their wealth decline visibly. Insurrections and revolts became increasingly frequent in Spain and brigandage widespread. Authority inspired little respect. Political persecution became ever more intense. Yet many army officers had absorbed liberal ideas during the wars and were out of sympathy with Ferdinand's conservative measures.

In most of Spanish America the years of Ferdinand's absolute rule were generally unhappy ones. He was obsessed with the idea of returning the colonies to the position they had occupied before 1808. He turned a deaf ear to the entreaties of even the conservative monarchs of France and Russia, who urged him to grant more autonomy to the colonies in order to preserve them. Ferdinand preferred a military solution. He dispatched General Pablo Morillo with an army of ten thousand veterans to Venezuela and Colombia in 1815. In Colombia the restored government executed five hundred patriots, including the scientist Francisco Caldas; and in Chile the Spanish military commander, exercising a despotic and arbitrary government, proceeded harshly to punish the Creoles, thus driving more and more of them into the camp of those who would eventually reassert independence. Whereas during the First War of Independence many could believe that loyalty to Ferdinand was consistent with constitutionalism and autonomy, such a belief was no longer possible.

The Spanish absolutists were in agreement with their liberal opponents on one thing: The ports of Spanish America must remain legally closed to all except Spanish trade. As one adviser to the king put it in 1817, "I would look upon the decree of free commerce as the same as the emancipation of America."[1] Where Spanish forces successfully reestablished colonial rule, the monopoly system was reimposed. In Caracas, for example, British imports had amounted to over £85,000 in 1812 but fell to just over £5,000 in 1815.[2] Creoles responded by launching a new wave of insurgency.

Only in Mexico was the situation different. Ferdinand sent an able

---

[1] Quoted by Timothy E. Anna, *Spain & the Loss of America* (Lincoln, Neb.: University of Nebraska Press, 1983), p. 172.

[2] Dorothy Burne Goebel, "British Trade to the Spanish Colonies, 1776–1823," *American Historical Review*, 43 (January 1938), 301.

viceroy there in 1816 who decreed a general amnesty and restored the unity of the viceroyalty. Although rebels still sporadically raided Spanish strongholds and interdicted roads, the years of relative peace were a welcome respite from the horrible bloodshed and destruction of the preceding years. The more radical Mexican Creoles found no audience when they spoke of independence; the masses had been cowed by superior Spanish forces, and the wealthy Creoles were reinforced in their conviction that Spanish rule spelled security.

Then European events gave another spin to the wheel. During January 1820 in Cádiz a mutiny broke out within an army being prepared for the American theater. The mutiny became an insurrection, and by March Ferdinand was forced to restore the Constitution of 1812. The liberals were once again in control and actually put the constitution's provisions into effect, even in Spanish America. Their hopes, however, of winning back the loyalty of Spanish Americans with liberal blandishments—which in any case did not include free trade—were doomed to failure. What the Spanish liberals failed to understand was that the ties between America and Spain had become frayed in 1808 when Napoleon usurped the Spanish throne; that many strands had been entirely broken in 1810, when the Central Junta disbanded, Spain appeared to be lost, and Spanish administrators failed to allow temporary self-rule in America; and that the remaining threads had been severed in the years after 1815, when Ferdinand, instead of establishing a kind of commonwealth with autonomy for each region in America, initiated his reactionary policies. Only massive force could have restored the old forms of Spanish power in America, and then only temporarily; but the Spanish liberals lacked the will to use massive force even if they could have marshaled it. The result was the rapid disintegration of what remained of the Spanish empire, as its agents who struggled to maintain it now lost their support from home and were even instructed to find an accommodation with the Americans against whom they had been fighting.

The Portuguese empire reached the same result by a somewhat different path. When the Portuguese court had departed for Rio de Janeiro in late 1807, a regency had been formally left in authority in Portugal. Napoleon's army had deposed it and fully occupied the country but soon found itself confronting resistance organized by local juntas. The arrival of a British army in mid-1808 gave these valiant Portuguese volunteers needed assistance, and victories against the French ensued. The regency was reconstituted, although real power rested in the hands of the British general William Carr Beresford,[3] who received the title of field marshal within the Portuguese army. By mid-1811 the French had departed Portuguese territory. Prosperity, however, did not return. Since Brazil was now economically independent of Portugal, the country's trade suffered sharp decline. With the defeat of Napoleon in 1814 people expected the return of the royal court. Instead, Brazil was raised to the level of a kingdom the next year, and King John VI (crowned in 1816) maintained Rio de Janeiro as his capital. Dissatisfaction with this state of affairs began to spread in Portugal. Beresford remained in control, resisting liberal innovations and even executing a popular military leader who espoused reformist principles. But, perceiving the direction of popular sentiment, he urged the king to return to Lisbon. Portuguese army officers who had fought to expel the French found it galling to be ruled from Brazil and have to take orders from an Englishman. Finally, the merchants who had expected a restoration of their former monopolies were sorely disappointed in the king's decision.

In August 1820 the army revolted in northern Portugal, and soon towns throughout the country joined in. A new constitution was rapidly drafted, modeled on the Spanish Constitution of 1812, seen everywhere as the fullest expression of liberalism. A Portuguese *côrtes* was elected. Its members reflected the liberal impulse of the merchant class in the port cities. The Côrtes summoned John VI home from Rio de Janeiro and, like its Spanish counterpart, attempted to reimpose colonial rule upon Brazil. The result was much the same: Brazilians now accustomed to running their own affairs would not tolerate a return to colonial status.

We may briefly complete the story for Europe. In Spain the absolutists were by no means silenced after the constitutionalist victory of 1820. They soon began plotting a counterrevolution and set up a kind of government-in-exile, claiming Ferdinand VII was a prisoner of the Cortes. The Spanish liberals, blind to their own danger, fell to fighting among themselves, with moderate and radical factions at one another's throats. Anarchy resulted. Ferdinand himself sent emissaries to France, Austria, Prussia, and Russia appealing

---

[3] Whom we earlier encountered in Buenos Aires.

for aid. These powers plus England had earlier—in 1818—vaguely considered a possible alliance to oppose revolutions, but England steadfastly refused to become entangled in the domestic affairs of countries on the Continent. In early 1823, however, Russia, Austria, and Prussia responded to Ferdinand's appeal by issuing an ultimatum demanding alterations in the Spanish constitution. The French wanted an opportunity to gain military glory and insisted in playing a part. So, just as Austrian armies had earlier put down revolutions in Italy, just so did French armies march into Spain in April 1823 to restore Ferdinand's absolute rule. The Cortes fled Madrid toward Cádiz, taking the king along. In areas taken by the French, fierce repression of all liberals followed. By late September all of Spain was occupied, and on October 1 Ferdinand was restored to his throne without a constitution. The regime that followed during the next ten years was even more retrograde than the one of 1814–1820. In Portugal as well an absolutist regime was reimposed in June 1823 under John VI. Ironically, this facilitated Portuguese recognition of Brazilian independence under a constitutional regime, since the new ruler of Brazil would be John's son Pedro and dynastic ties between Portugal and Brazil could be maintained.

One plan that surfaced in Spain in 1823—whether or not with full French agreement is unclear—was for Ferdinand's sisters to be crowned as rulers of Mexico and Peru, while another member of the Bourbon family would become king of Chile. The French navy would back them up, and French troops would be dispatched from Martinique. The French would also finance the outfitting of a Spanish expeditionary force. These hopes of reimposing Bourbon rule over the former colonies by relying on Ferdinand's allies, however, were frustrated by the British, who, having succeeded at last in opening Latin America's ports to their direct trade, were not about to allow the Spanish or their allies to close them once again. British diplomats had made their position clear to the European powers even before the French intervention. When Ferdinand issued an invitation for an international conference to consider allied help in restoring colonial rule, George Canning, the British foreign minister, replied that the British would not attend any conference in which free trade was in dispute. Aware of this British commitment, the United States rushed to issue the Monroe Doctrine in late 1823, declaring that European intervention in the Americas would be considered as an attack on the

United States, thus gaining credit for a policy that only England could enforce. Without fresh troops from Spain or her allies, the Spanish forces in Latin America were unable to hold out against the revolutionaries. As Canning later put it with much ethnocentric exaggeration, "I resolved that if France had Spain, it should not be Spain 'with the Indies.' I called the New World into existence to redress the balance of the Old."[4] From another point of view, however, it was at least equally the economic interests of Creole elites, the courage of the insurgents, and the leadership they enjoyed that forged an independent Latin America.

Leadership

Insurgent leadership during the Second War of Independence revealed marked contrasts as well as some similarities among the various countries of Latin America. Historians have traditionally attributed a great deal of importance to unique personalities, but it may be that it was not the individuals that produced the events but the other way around. Surely when similar events occur under differing leaders the importance of the person is at least thrown into question. A theory of revolutionary leadership cannot be developed here, but a few sketches may be useful before examining the events.

After Bolívar's flight from the chaos of Colombia in 1815, he remained undaunted and clear-eyed. From his haven in Jamaica he wrote one of the most famous documents of Spanish-American history (his "Letter from Jamaica"), in which he surveyed the origin and course of the revolution by region, analyzing the problems and prospects for the future, and then outlined his political philosophy, reasserting his commitment to establish freedom in South America. He believed that the people were unprepared for democratic procedures because the Spaniards had deprived them of governmental experience and that, therefore, a strong central government controlled by a powerful executive was the only alternative to anarchy.

But it was not so much his writing as his *machismo* that gained him

---

[4] Quoted by R. K. Webb, *Modern England: From the Eighteenth Century to the Present* (New York: Dodd, Mead, 1973), p. 167.

his leadership. The qualities of machismo—the ability to dominate, to impose one's will, to exercise charisma, and to display the qualities of a stallion both in derring-do and in attracting women—were, and still are, much admired in Latin America. Bolívar had them all. The attraction felt for him by the equally strong-willed Manuela Sáenz, sometimes called "La Libertadora del Libertador," exemplifies the trait. During a triumphal entry into Quito, Bolívar caught a wreath of flowers thrown from a balcony by this vivacious young woman. That night he met her at a ball, and from that moment on his fate was linked to hers; she often rode into battle with him, mounted astride rather than sidesaddle, as was then considered proper for women. Manuela expressed her nonconformist spirit in a letter to her English husband: "Do you think me less honored because he is my lover and not my husband? Ah, I do not live by the social preoccupations invented for mutual torment!"[5] When a dissident group tried to assassinate Bolívar several years later, Manuela held the assassins at bay with a pistol in each hand while he escaped through a window.

In Argentina another admirable although very different leader also arose: José de San Martín (1778–1850). The son of a Spanish civil servant in Argentina, his family had returned to Spain when the boy was young. At age eleven he had entered the Spanish army, eventually rising to a position of responsibility. Disgusted with events in Spain, he left and offered his services to the government of Buenos Aires in 1812, harboring a somewhat romantic attachment to the cause of independence. In Buenos Aires he became acquainted with the intellectuals, although he did not share their desire to transform the social structure. San Martín, unlike Bolívar, was reserved and unemotional, even cold, and womanizing was never attributed to him. In his campaigns he relied on careful planning rather than on improvisation. He did not particularly believe in Enlightenment reforms as did Bolívar, but limited himself to winning battles. He was not as great a soldier-statesman as Bolívar, but his virtues are nevertheless noteworthy.

In Mexico the new leader was Agustín de Iturbide (1783–1824), the son of a prosperous Basque immigrant. Iturbide was an officer in the Creole militia when Hidalgo's revolt broke out. Despite Hidalgo's entreaties, Iturbide scorned the movement and devoted his energies

---

[5] Quoted by Hubert Herring, A History of Latin America from the Beginning to the Present, 2d ed. (New York: Knopf, 1961), p. 268n.

José de San Martín, Liberator of
Southern South America

to quelling the revolt. For his efforts he was made military commander of Guanajuato in 1813 and there proceeded forcefully to
pacify the country. But his harsh means were inappropriate to the
purposes of the new viceroy, who was determined to win over the
opposition and create an enduring peace, so he was removed from his
command in 1816. Four years later, however, he was placed in charge
of an expeditionary force to eradicate the last focus of subversive
activity, the band of Vicente Guerrero. Instead of carrying out his
orders, Iturbide struck a bargain with Guerrero and declared for
independence, being careful to place himself at the head of the emerging new regime.

Instead of a colorful statesman like Bolívar or an austere military
planner like San Martín, Mexico at this juncture had only the self-
seeking Iturbide to lead it toward independence. Perhaps the defi-
ciency of leadership was related to the bitterness of the earlier social
protest, for it seems clear that a Mexican leader had to limit himself
to the goal of independence from Spain to be successful at that time;
when a leader took on the ideals of radical social change, he was
doomed to defeat. As the cause of independence was thus discredited,
it became the device of later opportunists rather than the creation of
heroic figures.

In Brazil two men together had the combined qualities of Bolívar:
one was José Bonifácio de Andrada e Silva (1763–1838), known
simply as José Bonifácio; the other was the prince regent, later Emperor Pedro I.

Left: Pedro I, Emperor of Brazil   *Right:* José Bonifácio de Andrada e Silva, Statesman of Brazilian Independence

José Bonifácio was born into a relatively wealthy family in São Paulo and was dispatched to Europe at an early age to complete his studies. He was greatly influenced by the Enlightenment, but like many European intellectuals, he was shocked by the excesses of the French Revolution and rather preferred "enlightened" England. After thirty years in Europe, he returned to Brazil and became Pedro's closest adviser in 1820. Recognizing that power must be restrained but fearing that the Brazilian people were not ready for an idealized republic, he sought the middle ground: a constitutional monarchy with restrictions on the power of the king. He believed these would preserve the monarchy. He fully deserves the title "Patriarch of Independence," for Bonifácio had the statesmanship of Bolívar.

Pedro had *machismo.* He subdued opponents by a mere look and impressed a nation of horsemen with his horsemanship. Despite having had little formal education, he was competent at languages, quickly grasped the intricacies of constitutional structure, and immediately perceived political advantage. He liked to think of himself as a liberal, and indeed was at ease with the masses, having been brought up among stable boys and palace servants, but he was an autocrat by temperament. At one time he cried, "Everything for the people but nothing by the people!"[6] Like Bolívar, Pedro was deeply affected by an illicit love affair. He made his mistress a marchioness and allowed her to sit at meetings of the Council of State. Pedro and Bonifácio together provided the leadership for independence.

Argentina and Uruguay

The restoration of Ferdinand VII to the throne of Spain in 1814 created problems in Argentina, for it brought long-postponed issues to a head. The accepted myth of loyalty to a dispossessed king was no longer tenable now that he was firmly reinstalled upon his throne. Thus Argentina would have to submit to Spanish rule or declare itself independent. If independence were to be declared, should the new nation be a monarchy or a republic? If a monarchy, who should rule? If a republic, should the government be centralized or federal? These questions could no longer be avoided and were the chief ones placed before the constituent congress that gathered at Tucumán in May 1816.

The congress declared the independence of the United Provinces in South America, but beyond this it was unable to proceed because the conservative delegates, greatly influenced by the now-prominent San Martín, desired a monarchy while Buenos Aires' liberals opted for a republic. In the meantime the congress appointed Juan Martín de Pueyrredón (1777–1850) as supreme director. He was a friend of San Martín, a monarchist, and a man of influence, having won fame in the battles against the British. Being a porteño, he was uneasy in the isolated vastness of the interior at Tucumán and soon persuaded the congress to continue its proceedings in Buenos Aires. For the next three years the congress deliberated while he directed a vain search for a king and, in effect, became the government.

Pueyrredón believed, as did the congress, that the new nation should include the territory that had formerly been part of the Viceroyalty of Río de la Plata. However, not only was Uruguay under the rule of Artigas, but the caudillos in the five provinces immediately to the north of Buenos Aires owed their allegiance to the Uruguayan

---

[6] Quoted in Neill Macaulay, *Dom Pedro: The Struggle for Liberty in Brazil and Portugal, 1798–1834* (Durham, N.C.: Duke University Press, 1986), p. 251.

leader. If Pueyrredón failed to win back these provinces and incorporate them into the nation, he would lose even the confidence of those provinces that had chosen him supreme director. Just before Pueyrredón assumed his new post, the government of Buenos Aires had entered into negotiations with the Portuguese in Brazil, inviting them to invade Uruguay. When Pueyrredón took his new post, he encouraged these negotiations, for he saw in them the opportunity to gain control over the other areas under Artigas' influence.

The plan worked well in eliminating Artigas. The Portuguese armies invaded Uruguay in August 1816 and occupied Montevideo by January 1817. Artigas threw all his resources, both those in Uruguay and those from his allied provinces, against the invaders, but his forces were vastly overshadowed by the veteran Portuguese armies. Still Artigas did not capitulate but for three more years continued a guerrilla campaign against the Portuguese until he was forced to seek refuge in Paraguay. The Portuguese were finally in control of Uruguay, and its independence was not secured until 1828.

Pueyrredón did not fare well, however, for although Artigas was no longer a threat, the other caudillos of the northern provinces continued to oppose him. These local leaders, who had emerged to power as a result of the breakdown of the old order, did not wish to bow once again to the hegemony of Buenos Aires and were also against the conservative ideology of the monarchists. Allying themselves with other caudillos of western Argentina, they unseated Pueyrredón in 1819. Practically every province—and sometimes a portion of a province—declared its independence as a sovereign republic. They thus plunged the nation into a ten-year period of recurring anarchy, which ended only when another caudillo, Juan Manuel de Rosas (1793–1877), came to power and forced the entrenched regionalists to yield to centralized authority.

During the Second War of Independence, the leaders in Argentina were less interested in legislative programs of social reform than before; nevertheless, the country did enter a period of social flux and mobility even in the west, and the power of the conservatives, who wished to maintain the old social structure, was undercut by the onslaught of ranchers and their rough cowboys. By 1820 the traditional society of fixed relationships was altered, and a monarchy would have been an anachronism. The liberal reformers in Buenos Aires, although unable to enforce their leadership on the country, could at least take comfort in that fact.

Venezuela and Colombia

In 1816 Bolívar returned to Venezuela from Jamaica via Haiti, where he had secured supplies in exchange for a promise to free the slaves of the mainland. Two new developments ensured his military victories over the next few years: foreign aid and the support or acquiescence of the poorer classes. The United States recognized Bolívar's belligerency, thus making it legal for American privateers, operating under various Spanish-American flags, to sweep the seas of Spanish shipping and isolate the Spanish armies; and English merchants, anxious to invade Spanish colonies with their goods, lent Bolívar more than £1 million, part of which he used to contract unemployed English, Irish, and Scottish veterans of the Napoleonic wars. By the end of 1817 Bolívar, with this new support, defeated the Spanish in the eastern llanos.

About this time the llaneros had a new caudillo, José Antonio Páez (1790–1873), Boves having died in battle. Páez came from a poor background and had been forced to flee to the llanos at the age of seventeen after having killed a man in his hometown, apparently in self-defense. At first a greenhorn, he had been hardened by the rough conditions and tough companions and gradually emerged as the leader of all the llaneros. At the end of January 1818 Páez met Bolívar and placed his followers under Bolívar's command. Páez was attracted to Bolívar by the latter's force of character, his vitality, his daring. But Bolívar had to offer more to Páez' followers. They demanded property, and Bolívar issued a decree that national lands—that is, those seized from the royalists—would be divided up among the loyal troops. With his now-augmented forces, Bolívar had complete control of the western llanos within a year.

Even earlier Bolívar had begun a systematic policy of incorporating pardo troops into his forces, promoting their leaders equally with whites according to their performance. Meanwhile, wherever the Spanish forces were victorious, they restored the old hierarchical society and reenslaved blacks. Morillo, the Spanish general, even demoted pardo officers whom Boves had privileged. Bolívar, moreover, now promised to free any slave who joined his army. Few thought military discipline and a soldier's harsh existence a great improvement over slavery, but at least they no longer fought against him. Bolívar had thus come to terms with the social reality of Venezuela.

Although the war in Venezuela was not yet won and no attempt had been made to take Caracas, Bolívar decided to push on into

Colombia. Just when the llanos were supposedly impassable because of the rains and military activity should theoretically have been at a standstill, his forces began a six-hundred-mile march from central Venezuela toward Colombia, wading in water up to the waist and swimming the horses. They then proceeded from the steaming low-lands up the narrow passes of the eastern slope of the Andes in intense cold. They slept in snow, covered only with tattered rags. At 12,000 feet many died from altitude sickness, and their horses perished from lack of food. Taking the Spanish completely by surprise in a rapid series of battles, Bolívar won a decisive victory on the plains near Bogotá at the battle of Boyacá on August 5, 1819. Although not a bat-tle involving many troops, it shattered Spanish morale. The viceroy in Bogotá fled ignominiously, and Bolívar marched along an open road into the viceregal capital to be welcomed by wildly cheering crowds.

Spanish reinforcements were prevented from leaving Spain by the liberal revolution of January 1820, and Pablo Morillo, the Spanish field commander in northern South America, received instructions to strike a truce. This he did and then resigned; he could not continue to maintain a colonial government if the armies at home were not interested. After the truce expired, Bolívar proceeded to mop up Spanish entrenchments along the northern coast. By June 1822 he had established the independence of most of Colombia and all of Vene-zuela with the exception of two minor enclaves, which remained under Spanish control.

Bolívar declared a general amnesty for all opponents, trying now to build a nation. He summoned delegates to one congress for both Venezuela and Colombia, for he wanted to make this one country. The delegates set up a centralized government to administer all of "Gran Colombia" through medium-sized departments and elected Bolívar president, but he immediately sought a leave of absence in order to pursue the war to the south and left Francisco de Paula Santander, the vice-president, in charge. Bolívar realized that until the Spanish were driven out of Peru, independence was not ensured anywhere in South America. His first target was Ecuador, for he wanted to include this area in Gran Colombia. Successful battles, especially those led by his chief lieutenant, Antonio José de Sucre, culminated in Bolívar's romantic entry into Quito in 1822.

Bolívar left behind him in Bogotá a government committed to Enlightenment principles and closer ties with England. Educational institutions were revamped to conform to British pedagogical ideas. The tax structure was redesigned in accordance with the latest economic theories. National courts with a uniform basis replaced the colonial judicial structure dependent on corporate and class divisions. Although the progress of these ideas was soon halted by political instability, turning back was now impossible.

Chile, Peru, and Bolivia

When San Martín was placed in charge of the Argentine Army in 1814, he soon perceived, as Bolívar saw later, that until the Spanish forces were crushed in Peru, the newly independent Argentine provinces would never be safe. And he had a new plan for how to do it. Instead of heading directly across the Andes for Lima, he would cross the Andes into Chile at a point where the ranges were relatively narrow, move across Chile to the coast, and go from the coast by sea to Lima to occupy the seat of Spanish power right away. Mopping up the highlands would then be a relatively easy task.

For three years San Martín prepared for the execution of his plan with the greatest care and attention to every detail while gathering his strength in western Argentina. In midsummer (January) of 1817 he led his fully equipped army of five thousand men—almost a third of whom were freed slaves—across the towering Andes into Chile. His move was preceded by elaborate feinting devices, so the Spanish army, caught unprepared, suffered a swift defeat. Then San Martín marched unhampered upon Santiago. With another major battle the next year he gained complete control of Chile's central valley. Chile thus gained its independence, and O'Higgins, who had joined San Martín in Argentina, was placed in charge of a government oriented toward progressive programs. O'Higgins also set to work marshaling resources for the next stage of San Martín's scheme.

Two years elapsed before San Martín was ready to move. For this part of the plan he needed a navy and a naval commander. The flood of unemployed British military personnel caused by Napoleon's defeat came to his aid. Few men in Europe had established a greater reputation for daring exploits than Thomas Cochrane, the future earl of Dundonald, and he was available for hire. San Martín sent an offer to Cochrane, who accepted. By 1820 all was ready. The army boarded the ships, and a fleet of twenty-three set sail toward the south of Lima. San Martín did not strike directly at Lima for he hoped to allow its citizens to rise up on their own; he did not want independence to be imposed upon an unwilling people.

By now news of the new liberal government in Spain had arrived in Peru. Liberal Spanish officers who had fought in the Peninsular War were dissatisfied with the lack of imaginative leadership demonstrated by the ultraconservative viceroy. Encouraged by the revolution in Spain, these officers deposed the viceroy and replaced him with a liberal, an action speedily approved in Spain. The new viceroy tried to reach a modus vivendi with San Martín, but San Martín was determined on complete independence, and the negotiations came to naught. The viceroy, the Spanish army, and most of the Spanish merchants then departed Lima, choosing as their base the rich interior with its silver mines and food-producing highland valleys. The cabildo of Lima seemed to welcome San Martín in July 1821.

San Martín's fatal flaw now became apparent: He would not undertake any operation unless entirely sure of success. The Spanish army in the interior easily outnumbered his, so he awaited developments. Without silver from the mines he could not pay his troops, finance his administration, or afford imports. Cochrane, claiming back pay and ever an opportunist, departed with the remaining war chest and sold his services to Brazil; and the army of Argentines and Chileans became restless and demoralized by the enforced inactivity far from home. San Martín himself was racked with pain caused by acute tuberculosis and took opium to escape the agony. His popularity waned, especially among people of property.

A year later San Martín met Bolívar at a secret interview at Guayaquil, Ecuador. What transpired is still unclear, but San Martín decided to leave the field and allow Bolívar to complete what San Martín had started. Back in Buenos Aires, despite his great achievements, San Martín was disowned by the liberals because of his conservatism and by the conservatives for his failure to rescue Pueyrredón's government when it was overthrown in 1819. Disillusioned, the man who had freed all of southern South America retired to Europe, where many years later he suffered a lonely death.

Bolívar assumed control in Lima in September 1823 but soon abandoned it, choosing a northern highland city as his headquarters. He took almost a year to consolidate his political power before facing the Spanish army in the interior of Peru. During this time the viceroy was having troubles of his own. When Ferdinand VII tore up the constitution, the viceroy's officers were divided. The Spanish forces in southern Bolivia were commanded by an archconservative general whose failure to receive recognition had apparently unbalanced his mind. The general now threw off the authority of the viceroy and declared that the area under his control would be an absolutist monarchy ruled by Ferdinand VII. The viceroy, finding entreaties useless, was forced to dispatch a desperately needed portion of his troops southward to overpower the general. Thus only a part of the Spanish army could confront Bolívar's forces. Bolívar won a clear victory in the interior of Peru in August 1824, and his troops, commanded by his lieutenant Antonio José de Sucre, then went on to defeat the Spanish army in the final battle of Ayacucho in December. Sucre next marched southward to clean up the remaining Spanish garrisons. A new nation emerged there in 1825, named Bolivia in honor of Bolívar. Sucre became its first president and attempted, valiantly but unsuccessfully, to create a modern nation tied into the European economic system. Bolívar in the meantime returned to faction-torn Lima to become chief executive of Peru and attempt to establish a stable government.

Factional bickering had broken out in Gran Colombia, however, and Bolívar soon returned there to try to maintain national unity and stability. But the forces of regionalism overwhelmed him at the same time as tuberculosis was sapping his energies. He died on December 17, 1830, on his way into exile. Three months before his death, Venezuela and Ecuador both declared their independence and shattered Gran Colombia. Manuela Sáenz, now scorned by the women of Bogotá who had once sought her favor, lived out her days in poverty. If Bolívar died sorrowfully, he is now remembered as much for his unflagging devotion to the cause of independence and his perceptive political theories as for his military role as the liberator of Venezuela, Colombia, Ecuador, and Peru.

Mexico

When a coalition of various elite groups in Mexico finally joined to establish independence, they did so in reaction to European events.

Perhaps in no other place in Spanish America did news of the Revolution of 1820 in Spain have a greater influence. Mexican conservatives still believed that the liberal promise of a modern secular state with individual freedom and mobility threatened all they held dear. But now the revolution in Spain had reestablished the ultraliberal Constitution of 1812; there was little reason to resist independence any longer, especially if it could be established under the aegis of a European king. The clergy, at least, openly preached against that constitution as a threat to religion. Meanwhile, Mexican liberals had come to the inescapable conclusion that without the support of the Creole aristocracy independence was a pipe dream. They welcomed the constitution, but they wanted to make it their own; no longer would they be dependent on the legislative measures of a Spanish parliament, the vagaries of royal fortune, or the whim of a Spanish viceroy. If support from conservatives for independence could be enlisted now, no matter what the reason, liberals must seize the day. Furthermore, neither conservatives nor liberals were happy with the Spanish Cortes' refusal to end monopoly trade, grant control over revenues to locally elected officials, or allow more than minority representation on the Cortes to the millions of Americans. Spain no longer appeared trustworthy to either group. Most important, the fact that the Indians and other workers now appeared quiescent made these elites confident that no social revolution would ensue from a declaration of independence.

The Second War of Independence in Mexico hardly deserves the name. When Iturbide was called upon to march against Vicente Guerrero, both conservatives and liberals were ready for a change. As he moved closer to the rebel chieftain, Iturbide embarked upon an extensive correspondence with various factions in Mexico City and Veracruz. Out of that exchange of letters emerged a manifesto calling for three basic provisions: independence under a constitutional monarch, preferably Ferdinand VII himself if he could come to America; a guarantee of religion, which meant much more than an established church and symbolized the acceptance of the divinely ordained corporate society as expressed in the fueros (specifically those of the militia officers and the clergy); and the end of any distinctions between Creoles and those Spaniards who joined the independent state. In this program there was something for everyone.

Iturbide struck a bargain with Guerrero, who joined the movement,

and their joint forces—dubbed the Army of the Three Guarantees—
set out for Mexico City. There were few battles to be fought. In most
places the potential opponents, led by Creole militia officers, were
beguiled by Iturbide's adroit use of propaganda and deserted to the
revolutionaries. Even churchmen preached sermons denouncing the
Spaniards and announcing that the war for independence would be a
religious war to defend the old order, and even the conservative city
of Puebla, led by the bishop himself, joined the movement. Many
Spanish soldiers in Mexico were as disheartened by the thought of a
colonial war as were the troops that had rebelled in Cádiz. When
Iturbide promised them safe conduct back to Spain, they eagerly
accepted it. He acknowledged the force of Mexican regionalism in
proposing home rule for each province. One by one most of the
cabildos voted to yield their allegiance to the new state.

In July 1821 a new viceroy, Juan O'Donojú, landed in Veracruz,
which, along with Mexico City, was one of the very few spots that
had not yet joined the revolutionaries. Quickly informing himself of
the situation, he signed a convention with Iturbide, agreeing to Mexican independence under the protective wing of Spain (indeed, the
Spanish Constitution of 1812 would be Mexico's at first). In September O'Donojú entered Mexico City by Iturbide's side. Together they
organized a provisional government, headed by a junta; O'Donojú
had a seat on the junta, and Iturbide became its president. Spain,
however, refused to sanction the actions of O'Donojú but could do
little about it, for only a couple of forts remained in Spanish hands.
Mexico was at last independent.[7]

Central America

Central America became free of Spanish colonial control only at the
time of Iturbide's revolt, for it formed part of the Viceroyalty of New
Spain. True, it had been a separate captaincy-general, named Guatemala. Included in it were what are today the countries of Costa Rica,
Nicaragua, Honduras, El Salvador, Guatemala, and Belize, plus the

---

[7] Although Spain would not recognize Mexico—or any other Spanish American
country—until after Ferdinand VII's death in 1833.

Mexican state of Chiapas and some parts of Yucatán. Thus it included a great variety of regions. In the sixteenth century the native inhabitants of the area that became Costa Rica had been relatively few, and the European settlers, in the absence of their labor, had to settle for small plots of land; by the nineteenth century it was predominantly European in ethnic background, and there had been little race mixture. At the other extreme, in Chiapas and Guatemala, a large population of Indians living in villages had provided abundant labor to the haciendas set up by the conquistadors, and by 1800 there was a sharp division between the white or mestizo urban residents and the communally organized villagers, most of whom still spoke no Spanish. El Salvador, Honduras, and Nicaragua fell somewhere in between, with a predominantly mestizo population. Along the low-lying Caribbean coast English loggers and settlers often allied themselves with the Miskito Indians and descendants of runaway black slaves from the Caribbean to harass the Spanish or to smuggle goods to the highlands.

Economic activities varied greatly from place to place, and social divisions were marked. The Creole hacendados of highland Guatemala mainly produced foodstuffs for the cities, relying both on draft labor from Indian villages and, increasingly, on debt peonage. The major exports to Europe were the dyes so important to the flourishing English textile industry. Dyewoods from the eastern tropical lowlands were taken directly by the British loggers on the coast. Indigo, produced by a labor-intensive process from the leaves of a bush, formed a growing part of the region's exports in the late eighteenth century, especially from the Pacific coast lowlands of El Salvador and Guatemala. Central American indigo faced growing competition from producers in South Carolina, Venezuela, and the East Indies; exports fell off by half between 1791–1800 and 1810–1819. Cochineal, the scarlet dye extracted from an insect, took its place. In general these products were produced by mestizo smallholders who fiercely exploited the Indians they brought down to lowland areas as draft laborers during the harvest season. Merchandising was handled entirely by the merchants of Guatemala City, who in 1790 succeeded in having their own guild established. The Bourbon-declared freedom to export directly to Spain instead of via Veracruz in Mexico had greatly benefited the dyestuffs trade. Merchants increasingly faced challenges for their control of the colony from a number of energetic immigrants from Spain and their children, who joined the Creole hacendados to form an aristocracy. This aristocracy predominated in the cabildo of Guatemala City. Regional divisions became exacerbated by diverging economic interests and were emphasized still further when the Bourbons in 1786 established separate administrations by appointing intendants in Chiapas, El Salvador, Nicaragua, and Honduras.

The events of 1808–1810 in Europe hardly sent a ripple though the established order in Central America. The Hidalgo revolt in Mexico City merely strengthened the resolve of the conservative forces to guard against liberal doctrines. But there were not many of those. The university faculty had long accepted the scientific approach of the Enlightenment, but few intellectuals followed the social and political theories of the French *philosophes*. Rebellions broke out in San Salvador and Nicaragua in 1811, but their only intent was to escape the control of the Guatemala City merchant guild; and a small conspiracy was uncovered in Guatemala City in 1813. Nothing more.

With the restoration of Ferdinand VII in 1814 the particularly conservative captain-general became even more intransigent. He supported the merchant guild against the cabildo at every step and seemed to consider every Creole a subversive. He especially cracked down on the smugglers who had been using the British settlements in Belize as a base. The Guatemalan weavers approved of his steps to exclude cheap British textiles, but those involved in the export trade chafed at the restrictions. His successor, appointed in 1818, was more easygoing, actually authorized some trade with Belize, and looked the other way when presented with evidence of smuggling. By then, however, the Creole aristocracy and the intellectuals were already forming an alliance and began to hammer out the lineaments of a reform program.

When Iturbide declared the independence of Mexico, he assumed that Central America, as part of the old viceroyalty, would be under his rule. The conservative Spanish element represented by the merchant guild thought otherwise and declared Guatemala's independence from Mexico. The Creole aristocracy retaliated, seizing power and leading Guatemala to vote for reannexation to Mexico. The mestizos of San Salvador then objected because they saw this move as a way of maintaining their subordination to Guatemala; only the intervention of a Mexican army finally subdued their revolt.

Subsequent events in Mexico initiated the long process through which five independent republics arose in Central America. When the Mexicans were unsuccessful in finding a European monarch who would accept the crown of Mexico, Iturbide seized it for himself in May 1822 as Agustín I. But his reign did not last long, and in March 1823 he was forced to abdicate by a coalition of federalists opposed to his centralizing tendency. This act changed the lineup in Central America. Now the Creoles, carrying the federalist impulse even further, saw the advantage of separation from Mexico and declared their independence that July as the United Provinces of Central America. Only Chiapas opted to remain in Mexico.

The ensuing history of the region is a turbulent one. The constitution adopted in 1824, like the Mexican one, created a federal nation with considerable autonomy for the states. It also enshrined many now-traditional liberal freedoms. The end of the Spanish trade monopoly meant that British cottons flooded the market while cochineal exports boomed; weavers went out of business, but the mestizo smallholders prospered. Slavery was abolished. The hacendados found the liberal trend unsettling, and the liberals unnecessarily created many enemies by feuding with the Church, encouraging the immigration of British settlers, transferring public lands into private hands, and imposing unpopular taxes. Despite a series of coups d'état and civil wars, however, the liberals endured for a number of years, until finally, in 1837, the peasant leader Rafael Carrera emerged to demand an end to their reforms. Leading both Indians and poor mestizos, he marched on Guatemala City. The government, now with its capital in San Salvador, was helpless to respond, and Carrera came to dominate Guatemala. It was at this point, in 1838, that Nicaragua, Honduras, and Costa Rica seceded. The separation of Guatemala from El Salvador had already been accomplished by default. This completed the process of independence in the area that had once been the old Viceroyalty of New Spain.[8]

Brazil

In Brazil the period from 1815 to 1820 was characterized by increasing friction between the Creoles and the Portuguese. The presence of the king in Brazil solved old problems but also created new ones. Fifteen

---

[8] Texas had become independent in 1836.

thousand courtiers had flooded the small town of Rio de Janeiro just when the Creole landowners began to find the city attractive for the first time. Many of the planters' town houses, rough-hewn though they were by European standards, were turned over to the courtiers; instead of gratitude, the courtiers evinced only spiteful and complaining scorn for the accommodations. Furthermore, the king gave all the best jobs in the administration to the Portuguese, which made a real point out of what had previously been a somewhat exaggerated rivalry between the Creoles and Portuguese, and issued edicts and instructions on matters that the members of the câmaras had long considered their exclusive concern. At the Congress of Vienna the Portuguese had been forced to join in forbidding the slave trade north of the equator and to promise to end it altogether eventually. But if this displeased planters, Portuguese merchants were made equally unhappy by the end of Brazil's colonial status, for now lesser Creole merchants and foreign merchants, especially British ones, competed with them openly and directly. Despite the prosperity that accompanied the reopening of European ports to Brazilian exports of sugar and cotton, dissatisfaction with the government grew. High taxes to pay for the army in Uruguay also exacerbated tensions. Separation from Portugal was no longer unthinkable because the king himself had made Brazil independent de facto and because many Spanish Americans, most notably those in neighboring Argentina, had declared their independence.

The presence of the king also exacerbated regional rivalries within Brazil. Previously each province had thought of itself as one colony among equals; now Rio de Janeiro and the southern provinces loomed much larger than the northeastern ones. The taxes collected by royal agents went not to finance Lisbon, but to develop the south. Thus the older northeastern provinces felt forgotten. When the king lingered on in Rio de Janeiro after the defeat of Napoleon, resentment became more intense. Then rumors swept the plantations that the king was considering abolishing slavery. In 1817 a short-lived, abortive revolution broke out in Pernambuco and neighboring provinces with the aim of creating an independent republic in that region. Its leaders were especially inspired by the French Revolution, despite their commitment to slavery. The movement presaged the coming struggle between centralists and federalists and between monarchists and republicans. The harshness with which the revolutionaries were treated after their capture alienated still more Creoles from the king.

As we have seen, in August 1820 the liberals in Portugal—primarily the businessmen most harmed by the end of the colonial relationship—following the lead of army officers and imitating their Spanish counterparts, revolted in behalf of a constitution. Portuguese troops in Belém and Salvador followed suit a few months later. The result was that the king would be circumscribed by a côrtes or parliament, and he was to return to Portugal. King John now faced a difficult dilemma: If he did not return to Portugal, he would obviously lose that throne, for even republican sentiment was not lacking there and certainly there would be other claimants to a vacant throne; if he did return to Portugal, he would probably lose Brazil, for the Creoles were fiercely jealous of their new proximity to the king. His solution was a typically Portuguese one: compromise. He sailed for Portugal in April 1821 (taking the treasury with him) but left his son Pedro as prince regent in Brazil with instructions, Pedro later said, to make himself king if formal independence should come.

John VI had no sooner arrived back in Lisbon than the Côrtes set out to reduce Brazil to colonial status. First, playing upon known regional rivalries, it issued regulations limiting Pedro's jurisdiction to southern Brazil and sent out governors for the other provinces. Next, it dispatched fresh troops to reinforce those in Salvador. Then it abolished the courts and other national institutions that the king had created in Brazil, appointed military governors to rule every province, and, finally, ordered Pedro back to Europe.

The result was almost inevitable, given the thirteen years of independent status Brazil had enjoyed. The Portuguese who surrounded Pedro in Rio de Janeiro urged him to obey the will of the Côrtes, as did the commander of the Portuguese troops and the Portuguese merchants. The Creoles, however, insisted that he remain in Brazil. Prominent among the latter was José Bonifácio, who got the câmara of his hometown of São Paulo to pledge support if the prince stayed. The Brazilian-controlled câmara in Rio de Janeiro did likewise. Even some Portuguese who had been in Brazil long enough to identify with their new country joined in the chorus. Pedro acceded to the Creoles' wishes in January 1822, thus defying the authority of the Côrtes he had sworn to obey. The Brazilian militia and Brazilian units of the army rallied to his defense, and this threat of force unnerved the Portuguese troops, who could see they were outnumbered. Expected reinforcements from Portugal did not arrive, and in February they sailed out of Rio de Janeiro harbor, moving to Salvador. Meanwhile, the Creoles in this latter city had also attempted a revolt, declaring their loyalty to Pedro, but suffered a defeat after four days at the hands of the disciplined Portuguese forces aided by that large segment of the militia there formed by Portuguese merchants.

In June Pedro summoned a congress to write a constitution for an autonomous kingdom, presumably still linked to Portugal. But in September he received dispatches from the Côrtes making clear that as far as it was concerned he would be subject to their every whim. Pedro also learned that an army of over seven thousand men was being readied in Portugal for transfer to Brazil. Brazilian autonomy had been as firmly rejected by the Portuguese Côrtes as the same proposal from Spanish Americans had been spurned by its Spanish counterpart. At this point, acting on advice from José Bonifácio, Pedro formally declared the independence of Brazil and soon crowned himself Emperor Pedro I, perhaps to reflect the fact that Brazil's various regions formed more than just one "kingdom."

But Salvador—as important a center as Rio de Janeiro—still remained firmly in Portuguese hands. The Creole sugar planters of its hinterland had declared their loyalty to Pedro and organized a provincial government of their own in an interior town, but whether they could continue to control their slaves was in doubt as the Portuguese now offered them freedom and some slave uprisings had already taken place. In July Pedro ordered a veteran French officer to join those planter-insurgents to help them organize their military effort. And the emperor now set about building up a navy (raising funds for it from a public subscription in which people made outright gifts of their jewels and silver) and placed it under the supervision of Admiral Thomas Cochrane, just "retired" from Chilean service. The Brazilian forces lay siege to the Portuguese garrisons in Salvador, allowing them no food. Brazilian civilians steadily fled the city to join the rebel forces, so that virtually only Portuguese merchants and soldiers remained. As long as these could be supplied by sea, they could hang on indefinitely, but when Cochrane's navy blockaded the port, they had no recourse but to surrender. They left for Portugal in July 1823. The same fate soon befell the remaining Portuguese garrisons in the northern ports of São Luís and Belém. Brazil was now entirely in Brazilian hands.[9]

---

[9] The Portuguese troops in Uruguay did not depart until March 1824, leaving only Brazilian ones or ones loyal to Brazil.

Yet Brazil in some ways was still not truly independent. For Pedro I was Portuguese, was still the legitimate heir to the Portuguese throne, and had many Portuguese advisers with him in Rio de Janeiro. Despite his liberal protestations, Pedro did not accept the principle that the people, and thus the people's elected delegates, were sovereign. When the congress undertook legislative measures that he opposed, adopted steps designed to exclude all Portuguese from positions of power (which by implication implied doubt about his own rule), and began drafting a constitution that, he felt, unduly circumscribed the monarch's power, he arbitrarily dissolved it. He then, in 1824, issued his own constitution, more conservative in tone than the one the congress had been discussing, although maintaining many of the same provisions and even expanding the list of individual rights. This constitution provoked immediate dissatisfaction among many Creoles, and a new revolt broke out in Pernambuco, whose leaders demanded the creation of provincial legislatures and the election of their own governor. The government put down the rebellion with exceptional violence and showed no mercy to the defeated partisans. Finally, Pedro often surrounded himself with Portuguese advisers, a practice that irritated the Creoles, especially by the end of the decade, when nativist sentiment against the Portuguese-born community reached a peak.

When John VI of Portugal died in 1826, Pedro had to decide what to do. Would he try to unite Brazil and Portugal once again? Or would he recognize that he could have neither throne without losing the other? This time compromise did not work. Pedro abdicated the throne of Portugal on behalf of his seven-year-old daughter (born in Brazil) and arranged her engagement to his brother, Miguel, whom he named regent. But Miguel soon usurped the throne for himself, and Pedro was forced to send aid to his daughter's Portuguese backers. Brazilian revenues were channeled into this dynastic quarrel, which to most Brazilians seemed irrelevant and outdated.

There were still other reasons for dissatisfaction with Pedro's rule. Chief among these was the sad defeat in Uruguay. After the success of the Portuguese armies in 1820, Uruguay had been given all the trappings of a Brazilian provincial government, but the real power resided in the army of occupation. Although a large part of this army departed for Portugal after Brazil became independent, the Brazilian contingent, that is, soldiers of whatever origin but loyal to Pedro I, was large enough to maintain Uruguay under Brazilian control at first.

In 1825, however, thirty-three Uruguayan patriots landed from Argentina, and local dissidents rose up in revolt to greet them. New juntas were formed and declared their willingness to join Argentina, giving it an excuse to send in its troops to help their cause. The Brazilians suffered repeated defeats until only Montevideo remained in Brazilian hands two years later; Argentina controlled the rest. The British, whose trading interests were suffering from the warfare, then stepped in to moderate the quarrel and in 1828 forced both contenders to grant Uruguay independence as a buffer state between them. Both the Argentine and the Brazilian governments lost prestige at home, and Pedro was discredited as a military leader.

Finally, as the price of British diplomatic recognition, Pedro was compelled to end the slave trade by 1830. Legislation to that end was drafted, and tensions mounted. The Creole landowners, who formed the dominant economic class, believed that the basis of the country's prosperity would thereby be destroyed and that they would be plunged into poverty if no more slaves could be brought in from Africa. They blamed him, rather than the British.

Thus, after Pedro's declaration of independence, nearly all his subsequent policies had turned the Creole upper and middle classes against him. Even the economy had turned sour as Cuban sugar and North American cotton now undercut Brazil's products, and coffee was only beginning to be an important export commodity. Finally, in April 1831 a mob, backed by the Creole militia, marched on the royal palace; Pedro I had no other choice but to give in and sail for Europe. But elite Creoles also feared republican anarchy, so rather than moving in that direction they forced Pedro I to abdicate in the name of his five-year-old Brazilian-born son (also named Pedro) and leave him behind. He could be brought up according to norms more suitable for this American empire, and he was to have as tutor José Bonifácio. Regents chosen by a Brazilian parliament would rule during the boy's minority. One point he would thoroughly absorb was that elite Creoles must be treated with the greatest circumspection. At last Brazil was being run by Brazilians. In this sense independence was complete in Brazil only in 1831.

*   *   *

The unity of Brazil was ensured then and later by the legitimacy bestowed on the central government by the royal presence. Whether in the person of John VI, Pedro I, or the younger Pedro, Brazil had a king. Regional rivalries were intense and in the next several years erupted in several separatist movements. But the fact that the majority among the elite accepted these kings' right to rule—combined with the fear of a civil war in a society so dependent on slaves—largely explains why this huge country remained one. Of course, not just any king would do; Mexico, like Brazil, adopted a monarchical form of government, but the emperor of Brazil was a legitimate heir of an ancient dynasty, whereas the Mexicans were unsuccessful in attracting Ferdinand VII or any of his relatives and had to settle for Iturbide, who could make no such claim. No wonder Colombians, Argentines, Bolivians, and others hoped, at one time or another, for a European monarch. Even with that legitimacy, Pedro I was deposed in the end.

Other dissimilarities must also be taken into account. If the king of Spain had come to America, it is doubtful that he could have maintained the allegiance of all the Spanish colonies; that is, there was apparently a greater preexisting unity in Brazil than in Spanish America as a whole, partly because of geography, partly because of better communications. The fact that the intellectuals of Brazil, or at least its lawyer-jurists, had by necessity all received their training at the same university in Portugal created in them a common outlook on power and loyalty to the state plus personal acquaintance with their counterparts in other regions. The Spanish Americans had had numerous universities in which to study, usually in their own regions.

A major point of difference is that in Brazil the traditional, corporate society suffered much less disturbance than in most of Spanish America. Major social changes had been wrought by years of warfare in Spanish America, whereas within Brazil real fighting had occurred only in and around Salvador. It is probably not coincidental that, within Brazil, only in the Salvador region did slaves believe it possible to strike for their freedom. Nothing resembling the Hidalgo revolt took place there.

Still, there were also major points of similarity between Spanish and Portuguese America. Everywhere the key figures during the independence movement were the Creole landowners, and their desire for power impelled them increasingly to reject peninsular authority. During the First War of Independence the Creoles of both areas had the experience of being ruled from a capital within their own borders. After that war the insensitive behavior of the Spanish Cortes and Portuguese Côrtes increased the tensions between themselves and the Creoles. At some point in both areas Creole militias found it useful to make a show of force. The British interest in opening the ports played an important role in the independence movement generally, and both Spanish and Portuguese merchants, who had once monopolized international commerce, suffered thereby. Regional tensions rose in Brazil as in Argentina, Chile, Colombia, and Mexico. Almost everywhere potential unrest on the part of African slaves, free blacks, Indians, or mestizos played an important part in shaping the actions of the elites.

Chapter Six
The Meaning of Independence

How significant were the changes wrought by the wars of independence? Bolívar concluded that he had "ploughed the seas,"[1] and other participants probably felt the same disillusionment. Subsequent historians have sometimes similarly observed that the main problems Latin America faced in 1810—underdevelopment, arbitrary and unrepresentative government, ignorance, exploitation, social injustice—are the same ones it faces today and that nothing has really changed in nearly two centuries, much less in those fifteen years of revolution. But to begin along a road is often as difficult a step as to reach its end. And many of the adversities of Latin America today are basically problems emerging precisely from the region's inclusion in the world capitalist system, from the incompatibility of Enlightenment principles with preexisting values, and from the unresolved social tensions that began surfacing at the time of independence. In short, independence (and the Bourbon reforms that preceded and to some extent heralded it) signified a basic altera-

---

[1] Quoted by Gerhard Masur, *Simon Bolívar* (Albuquerque: University of New Mexico Press, 1948), p. 687.

136

tion in direction. The movement's importance cannot be seriously denied.

Inclusion in the World Economy

Independence, after a period of recovery from the wars, fostered a closer integration of all Latin America into the world economy. National elites welcomed the expanding forces of industrial capitalism centered in England and with them social and intellectual changes as well. Imports from northern Europe and exports thereto multiplied rapidly. This kind of change concomitantly produced an expansion of plantation agriculture and cattle raising to supply the expanding needs produced by Old World manufacturing development and urbanization. The onslaught of cheap European manufactured goods simultaneously destroyed ancient craft industries in Latin America. Latin American cities began to look to northern Europe for models, and the gap between the cities and the countryside became more noticeable. Plantations drew more workers into the wage-earning sector, weakening communal village life. Moreover, the areas that were more closely tied to overseas trade emerged to prominence while old ones declined still further: Argentina and Brazil became the dominant areas of South America, ousting Peru from a position it had long held and has never regained. The widening currents of European influence eroded the walls of conservatism and traditionalism and opened up channels for the circulation of fresh ideas. In summary, independence advanced processes begun in the eighteenth century, although regional variations continued to affect the rate of change.

The opening of the ports was the most concrete example of the new regimen. As a British businessman in Buenos Aires recalled in the 1820s:

> On a free trade being tolerated by the viceroy in 1808, it was at once seen that the country was in every respect fitted for great commercial improvement; and on being thrown open altogether in 1810, it was very soon carried to an extent altogether unknown in former times: for the barriers of exclusive privilege and monopoly being once thrown down, the commerce of the country advanced at a pace beyond all example.[2]

---

[2] Quoted in R. A. Humphreys (ed.), *British Consular Reports on the Trade and Politics of Latin America, 1824–1826* (London: Royal Historical Society, 1940), pp. 31–32.

In Brazil the value of British goods imported directly went from just a little over £1,000 in 1806 to over £2,000,000 in 1812 and to over £3,000,000 in 1818; in Argentina it went from £369,000 in 1812 to £1,104,000 in 1824; in Mexico from £21,000 in 1819 to more than £1,000,000 in 1825; and in Chile from £37,000 in 1817 to nearly £400,000 in 1822. The importation of English textiles into Buenos Aires jumped from 3 million yards in 1814 to 15 million in 1824.

Hopes of exporting vast quantities of Latin American produce to northern European markets were frustrated in many places by the damages inflicted by the war. British businessmen reported, for instance, that in Uruguay the "invasion by the Brazilians . . . completed the ruin which Artigas had begun. Accordingly these once flourishing provinces are now exceedingly poor; the immense herds which in former times covered their rich pasture grounds have entirely disappeared."[3] The possibility of exporting from Chile to Europe had never been great, and exports continued to be principally minerals—especially the silver the Chileans earned by trading with Peru and Bolivia. The exports from Peru were chiefly precious minerals, and, after the first rush to exchange accumulated supplies for the newly cheap imports, silver was in relatively short supply compared to colonial days because of the wartime destruction of the mines. In Venezuela the conflict similarly resulted in abandoned estates or only partially cultivated plantations because a large proportion of the slaves had been freed or had fled. On the other hand, exports, however limited, were no longer funneled through a parasitic mother country. Whereas in 1820 Mexico shipped practically all its exports to Spain, by 1823 only a tenth of them went there.

Within Spanish America only in Argentina did the new trading opportunities immediately lead to export wealth. With British ships ready to carry away its livestock products, Buenos Aires province prospered, despite the absence of Peruvian silver from its export lists. Pastoral activity even replaced farming near the city, and flour came to be imported. With Uruguay and Venezuela temporarily unable to compete, investment opportunities blossomed. Argentine governments granted public lands in huge tracts through long-term leases (eventually converted to private property). In Buenos Aires province

---

[3] Ibid., p. 40.

the hegemony of merchants was now replaced by that of ranchers. And they needed relatively few workers to produce thousands of valuable hides, hundreds of barrels of tallow, and tons of jerked beef. The gaucho, who had once roamed free, was soon reduced to a peon, circumscribed by laws against vagabondage and forced into a position of deference and humility before the ranch owners.

The new trading relationships with overseas nations deeply affected commercial patterns. Independence ruptured the old family connections between Iberian merchants in the colonies and their relatives in Spain and Portugal, and trade quickly became the speciality of the British, who had the necessary contacts with suppliers and a large merchant marine. Just eight months after the opening of Brazilian ports, 150 British traders had installed themselves in Rio de Janeiro. Internal patterns also altered. The British consul in Mexico reported that "formerly the principal and most opulent merchants of New Spain were established in the city of Veracruz. They were either old Spaniards or their immediate descendants." These merchants had sold to wholesalers in Mexico City, who distributed imported goods to retailers around the country. But as the British "are almost exclusively commission merchants they find it more advantageous to supply directly the retailers. They have, therefore, all established themselves in the City of Mexico."[4] Similar alterations in channels and procedures doubtless occurred throughout the continent. Many Spanish and Portuguese merchants were driven out of Latin America by the sporadic mob violence that targeted their countinghouses, as happened in Chile as early as 1812, in Brazil in 1824, and in Mexico in 1827 and 1829. Latin Americans with capital preferred to invest in land or other productive ventures rather than in trade. Certainly British merchants were ready to take their place in every Latin American trading center.

If we compare the foreign trade of the various parts of Latin America, it becomes apparent that four factors affected the growth in the volume of exports and imports. First, and most important, was the presence or absence of resources suitable for introduction into the international economy. Second was the existence of a commercial structure adequate to exploit this potential, including, especially,

---

[4] Ibid., pp. 302–303.

merchants with sufficient capital and mercantile know-how. Third was the difficulty or ease of transporting raw materials to the European consuming centers and manufactured imports to the Latin American population. Fourth was the degree to which military operations had left the resources, the commercial structure, and the means of transportation unscathed. By any one of these measures, Brazil comes out ahead. Just at the time of independence, coffee began to be planted there on a large scale. Rich Portuguese merchants were gradually superseded by the British without any shock to the commercial system (a few Englishmen had already been present before independence). Both the new coffee areas and the older sugar ones were near the coast, and independence had been won virtually without warfare. Thus one can see that although the shift in direction of Latin American economic life toward northern Europe was a secular process principally impelled by changes occurring in the Old World, its specific effect depended upon the particular conditions in each part of Latin America. On the other hand, all of Latin America was heading in the same direction, even if at a different pace.

Since independence Latin American governments have often found themselves heavily dependent on foreign loans, principally because of their inability to tax the major sources of internal wealth (in some places the elites equated taxation with the tyranny of the colonial system) and their exaggerated optimism regarding future revenues. The pattern began during the Second War of Independence, when the authorities sent agents to London to negotiate bond issues with bankers. The agents varied in effectiveness but eventually succeeded in raising several major loans. The Colombian agent sent by Bolívar, for instance, negotiated for £2 million in 1822. By 1825 Latin American governments had borrowed over £21 million in England, of which £7 million was for Mexico, £6.7 million for Colombia, £3.2 million for Brazil, £1.8 million for Peru, and £1 million for Chile. A large part of these loans was taken up in commissions and fees to the banks, and only some £12 million was actually netted from them for government expenditures. As the Latin American agents who negotiated the loans were not always wise in their use, even less than this sum actually reached Latin America. By 1827 every Latin American bond issue was in default, although Brazil resumed payments in 1829. It was not until the 1860s that British investors again showed any willingness to buy Latin American government bonds. Through this experience the relationships between Latin Americans and Britishers became closer, though not necessarily more cordial.

Private investment followed trade, and foreign capital came to dominate the Latin American economy. The news of the final defeat of Spanish armies in 1824 led London investors immediately to speculate in fly-by-night mining companies designed to exploit the fabled riches of Spanish America from Mexico to Bolivia. Some £3 million was invested in such ventures. But neither the welcoming governments nor the investing community was mature enough at that time to overcome the challenges presented by the Latin American terrain, climate, backward transportation, and traditional attitudes. One company, the Potosí, La Paz and Peruvian Mining Association, sent out four representatives to initiate its operations. They consumed a large part of the company's initial capital of £50,000 in luxury provisions for their travels, including, according to a participant, "gingerbread nuts and peppermint drops."[5] The machinery, tools, quicksilver, furniture, supplies, and skilled workmen never even reached their Bolivian destination, and the agents, for lack of further funds from London, were eventually forced to sell their clothing, watches, and jewelry to survive. Most such companies went bankrupt, but the precedent was set for later investments on a much larger scale that proved more successful.

Closer ties with northern Europe meant alterations in lifestyle for many Latin Americans. The centers of culture began to look increasingly to northern Europe for everything. Just as many an exquisite, superbaroque architectural decoration had been chiseled away in the late eighteenth century to comply with current European aesthetic standards, just so the clothing styles of the Europe-oriented cities now varied according to Parisian fads or London customs. Even the furniture and diets of those in the cities were affected. In Brazil, for instance, wheat flour progressively replaced manioc and cornmeal as an urban food staple. These tendencies were especially noticeable in the larger cities and thus served to further differentiate urban from rural life in Latin America.

All these changes proceeded at an even faster pace after about

---

[5] Quoted by William Lofstrom, "Attempted Economic Reform and Innovation in Bolivia under Antonio José de Sucre, 1825–1828," *Hispanic American Historical Review*, 50 (1970), 293.

midcentury, once the international economy had settled down to the patterns that were to characterize it until World War I. Impelled by technological developments, especially in transportation, the lifting of tariff barriers in Europe, the large-scale migration of European peoples, and the mobility of capital, Latin America was swept ever further into the European vortex. As the political instability that had characterized the first half of the nineteenth century diminished, economic growth increased. British manufactures sent to Latin America skyrocketed once railroads extended the orbit of European commerce far beyond the ports. Massive investments in rails, mines, urban services, cattle ranches, and other enterprises characterized the latter half of the century. The United States followed in England's footsteps. With these investments, of course, went power. Although to listen to the plaintive complaints of the investors their lot was one of constant harassment by hypernationalistic governments, the more common attitude among many government officials was rather one of sycophantic pleading interspersed with sly acquisitive suggestions.

It is not surprising then that postindependence Latin American economies have often been labeled "neocolonial." It seemed as if the economic place of Spain was now held by England or, later, by the United States. The subsequent struggle to industrialize is therefore often considered still another war of independence. And since much of the early industrialization of Latin America was financed by foreign capital and directed by foreign management so that every action of the governments to tax, restrain, or inspect these economic interests ran aground on the power of foreign governments, many Latin Americans came to believe that true independence requires industrialization under national control, carried on by the state if necessary.

Changing Ideology

The transformations initiated during the eighteenth century were greatly speeded up by the independence movement. Although the hierarchical society can hardly be said to have been destroyed, it was now under heavy attack. Its corporate structure was as threatened by the removal of the king as a family's cohesiveness is by the death of a father. The complex layering of craft guilds, Church corporations, racial groups, and propertied classes was shaken up by these events and would never be the same. Political and economic liberalism opened the way for the individual to break out of the bonds of his social origin and rise—or sink—according to other criteria. Although not completed then or later, the process had been hastened.

The chief intellectual burden of the independence movement was liberalism—the release of the individual from the binding force of a static, stratified social structure. This liberalism was still chiefly informed by the Enlightenment, and the concept of natural rights was paramount within it. Latin American thinkers considered freedom of speech, the press, religion, and association basic to any governmental system. They believed that constitutions were necessary to restrain the government and lay down the rules of the game for everyone, and that the separation of powers would ensure their execution.

Everyone was now a citizen. The creation of an overarching loyalty to nations, to substitute for or at least subsume the multiple loyalties to corporations (guilds, brotherhoods, villages, provinces), took place only gradually. At the same time, whereas in the old regime power had been delegated downward from the king, now sovereignty was conceived as emanating from "the people." In building this new unified loyalty, this sense of common participation in a nation, the state played an important if not predominant part. Similar transitions had occurred and were occurring elsewhere; it was probably easier where there were already strong states, as in northern Europe, or where a tradition of popular representation had been established, as in British North America. In Latin America it would be a slow and arduous process.

The failure fully to implement these reforms stemmed not so much from the alleged reluctance of the new leaders to impose strong government but from their refusal to come to terms with the landowners and other privileged social groups they encountered—that is, with the forces of traditionalism. O'Higgins, for instance, was a forceful executive who accepted the necessity of centralized power. He strengthened the police, captured bandits, encouraged trade, killed his opponents or sent them into exile, intervened in elections, and attempted to perpetuate himself in power. But he also abolished entail, attacked the Church, ignored titles of nobility, and tried to break down the ancient barriers between the classes. That is why O'Higgins' regime was relatively short-lived.

Other reformers met with similar failures. Bernardino Rivadavia in

Proclamation of the Portuguese Constitution (1820) in Brazil

the province of Buenos Aires, for instance, was a fanatical liberal. A disciple of Bentham who believed that the general good could be achieved principally by shrinking the state and inattentive to the structural forces working against him, he attempted to strengthen the freedom of the individual through legislation. He tried to encourage immigration from northern Europe, but the cattle ranchers of the region were not interested. He attacked the Church, eliminated the compulsory tithe, and tried to control the movement of clergymen, apparently unaware of how such measures offended the common people, over whom the clergy exercised much influence. He wanted to attract foreign capital for industry in an area that lacked coal or iron, adequate transportation, and a decent consuming market. He wanted to lessen import duties and rely instead on taxes on income and land in a society dominated by wealthy landowners, who were already tired of financing the wars. Yet for the lower classes he had only contempt. He advocated giving ranchers clear title to public lands, but he saw the gauchos who were being closed out of the open range merely as lazy vagabonds whom he wished to draft into the army or assign to compulsory public works. Freedom was for the success-ful. His tenure as a kind of prime minister in the provincial government lasted only from July 1821 to April 1824 and that as president of a chimerical United Provinces of the Río de la Plata from February 1826 to July 1827, when the union broke into its component parts.

Valentín Gómez Farías, president of Mexico from 1832 to 1834, also attempted to impose the values of the Enlightenment upon his reluctant countrymen. Society, he believed, consisted of atomistic individuals who should be free to rise or fall according to their abilities, and the state's responsibility was principally to ensure that freedom. A physician by training, he believed that every problem had a rational answer. He abolished state monopolies, ended the fueros of all corporate groups, revoked the compulsory payment of Church tithes, and stripped the Church of its educational responsibilities, creating secular institutions of higher education. The devout common people were bewildered by his anticlericalism, the vested economic interests were alienated, and the army bemoaned the loss of its fuero. He was overthrown by a coup after two years in office.

The major contribution of this generation was to elaborate a program and spell out its meaning in concrete acts. These men wished to expand educational facilities because only in this way could humans control nature and society. They tended almost invariably to separate Church and state because they saw that union as one of the major bulwarks of the hierarchical society.[6] They also identified the Spanish heritage as a bad one. It was, so they alleged, the chief cause of all Latin America's evils. If they were right, then they may be considered prophets of doom despite their optimism; for the Iberian heritage is all they had.

One should not exaggerate the degree to which Latin Americans copied standards of government from other areas. Glen Dealy, the political scientist, has provocatively explored the degree to which a Thomistic and colonially derived political theory was maintained in the early constitutions of Latin America.[7] John Locke's views and Anglo-Saxon political institutions were not as widely adopted in Latin

---

[6] By eliminating the king, the independence movement had already brought about this separation in thought if not in legal fact. Cut loose from this restraining force, the Church in the nineteenth century was often as irresponsible in its actions as the army was. Change rather than stagnation lay behind these developments.

[7] Glen Dealy, "Prolegomena on the Spanish American Political Tradition," *Hispanic American Historical Review*, 48 (1968), 37–58.

America as is usually thought. The common good was to be achieved not by the satisfaction of conflicting interests and the balancing of powers but through the morality of leaders. Uniform religious education, divine guidance, and control of speech and press were to be used to foster this morality. Many constitutions even embodied a board of censors to watch over the virtue of officials, and the constitutional qualifications for office sometimes included moral ones. Of course, in correcting one exaggeration one must not fall into another and suggest that the new political system could not be differentiated from the old one.

The political theory of the time may also be studied in the thought of Bolívar. Deeply concerned with the nature of Spanish-American society, he was a political philosopher of no small importance. He always reiterated that "the excellence of a government is not in its theory, its form, or its mechanism, but in being appropriate to the nature and character of the nation to which it is applied."[8] Many of Bolívar's contemporaries believed that the rights of the individual could best be defended from the arbitrary action of the state if the central government were kept weak, the executive power curtailed, and state and local government exalted, whereas he believed in a powerful executive within a strong central government. Weak government, he thought, would lead to anarchy and anarchy to dictatorship; it was better to have a strong government to begin with, placed within the legal structure, than to end up with a strong government anyway, but under a tyrant. He recognized that the only alternative to the centralization established by the Spanish crown was indefinite division. A strong executive, he said, would suit the Spanish-American experience, but not a monarchy, for the clock could not be turned back. Many of his ideas later came to be commonplace in Latin America.

But despite these evidences of Latin American willingness to synthesize a new view of humankind with those inherited from Spain, the most important feature of the period was precisely the change in direction. It moved toward a conception of society as being made up of individuals. Everywhere one finds the gradual replacement of the

---

[8] Quoted in Guillermo Morón, *A History of Venezuela*, John Street (ed. and tr.) (London: Allen & Unwin, 1964), p. 128.

corporate judicial system by a uniform national court structure. And although individual freedoms were often curtailed, they were also given a recognition never seen in colonial days. Rituals reflect the change: No longer did elaborate religious processions with each corporate group ranged in its hierarchical order give visual expression to a society of estates. Now central plazas in which trees were newly planted afforded citizens a supposedly egalitarian gathering place, although it was the newly affluent upper middle class of "proper" people who strolled there on Sundays.

The same principles undergirded the changes in economic life. The simplification of the tax structure is a good example of this. Instead of multiple rates on different articles of trade, monopoly contracts, Indian tributes, internal trade barriers, and special taxes to finance the operation of various corporations like the merchant guild, the tendency was now toward the creation of relatively uniform duties on imported goods (intended not as protective tariffs but as sources of revenue). The simultaneous but more gradual adoption of laissez-faire practices, that is, the removal of government restrictions upon economic activity, also resulted from the new ideology. Much later such practices came to be identified with conservatism since they ignored the needs of the mass of people, who seldom benefited from them, but in the first half of the nineteenth century they were seen as radical innovations and hailed by those who wished to foster change. Those reformers could not have been expected to know that when superimposed on the still remaining hierarchical and elitist traditions, these policies would mean merciless exploitation.

Social Tension

The new ideology was an imported one. In its origins, as we saw in Chapter One, it had emerged from a virtual social revolution. In England and France the violent phases had come only after a long period of gestation in which a new class had gathered its strength. No such process occurred in Latin America. A few wealthy and a great mass of poor, with only a minute (though growing) middle class, continued to characterize Latin American societies. Political liberalism in such a society meant that liberty was for the few at the top. Yet the efficacy of a free enterprise system depends on a relatively even distribution of wealth. Lifting price controls on food, for instance, should theoretically provoke suppliers to increase production and thus keep prices down; but if only a few own land it merely encourages price gouging. With only few employers, labor is helpless to bargain. Independence simply meant that a narrow elite increased its political control. On the whole, the social groups whom the well-off had feared in the eighteenth century made few gains as a result of independence; many of them actually lost ground.

Certainly the Indians suffered under the new regime. Although steadily exploited for three hundred years, they had also been protected by the Spanish system. The Indians had had certain corporate rights, privileges, and exemptions that the new Latin American leaders wished to destroy. The reformers argued that if the Indians were forced to sink or swim as a result of their own initiative and hard work, they would emerge from their subhuman condition, shake off their alleged lethargy, and participate more fully in national life. The new legal systems emphasized private property rather than communal holdings, which many thought should be completely forbidden. But instead of the expected results, the individualism of the new era exacerbated the exploitation of Indians by those better equipped for that kind of struggle.

On the other hand, many leaders now considered outright slavery inimical to the interests of society, as it restricted the free initiative of the individual. Outside Brazil the gradual end of slavery was almost invariably one of the goals of the independence leaders, even if only vaguely envisioned or laxly pursued.[9] Most Spanish-American countries declared that all children born after a certain date would be free, although they all required that such a child should continue to serve the mother's master for a fixed term of fifteen to twenty-five years. As well, they all ended the slave trade. As for freeing slaves, the most common proposal at first was to offer freedom in exchange for military service. In Argentina, where approximately 8 percent (30,000) of the population had been enslaved when the independence movement began, the revolutionary governments required many slaveowners to sell their human property to the state for use in the armies. If the draftees survived the war and fought for five years, they

---

[9] Hidalgo and Morelos both decreed the outright end of slavery.

would be free. San Martín relied heavily on this expedient, and his reputation went before him: In Peru the viceroy reported in 1818 that slaves had "openly decided for the rebels, from whose hands they expect liberty."[10] Bolívar, as we have seen, after his visit to Haiti pursued the same policy in Venezuela, arguing that it was unfair that free men should die for freedom while slaves lived on as slaves. Although he later urged the legislatures of Venezuela and Colombia to abolish slavery altogether, he had his doubts in Peru, where he declared that "if the principles of liberty are too rapidly introduced, anarchy and destruction of the white inhabitants will be the inevitable consequence."[11] In any case the slaveowners naturally objected to abolition, and it did not occur in Argentina, Venezuela, Colombia, or Peru—all of which had substantial numbers of slaves—until the 1850s (in contrast to Chile, which declared the end of slavery in 1823, and Mexico, where slavery ended in 1829). Everywhere it was argued that freeing the slaves would encourage social disruption.

After Haiti, the country of the Americas that in colonial times had most depended on slaves was Brazil. José Bonifácio argued for their freedom on the ground that slavery impeded the social peace necessary for a powerful state. But hardly anyone listened to him on that score. The presence of thousands of slaves had much to do with tempering the subsequent fervor of those who advocated republicanism or provincial separatism, for such movements often opened opportunities for revolts that slaves quickly seized. Brazil did not abolish slavery until 1888, a year before adopting a republican form of government. And it is not coincidental that Cuba, another area where slave labor formed the backbone of the economy and where slavery did not end until 1886, did not become independent from Spain until 1898. Fear of repeating the Haitian experience made slaveowners extremely cautious when contemplating political upheaval.

There were other social changes in Latin America as well. Colonial restrictions upon freedmen were removed in most of Latin America, and blacks and mulattos were now on an equal legal footing with other

---

[10] Quoted by Timothy E. Anna, *The Fall of the Royal Government in Peru* (Lincoln, Neb.: University of Nebraska Press, 1979), p. 151.

[11] A British consul quoted in Peter Blanchard, *Slavery and Abolition in Early Republican Peru* (Wilmington, Del.: Scholarly Resources, 1992), p. 10.

citizens. That does not mean they were treated equally, for social and economic discrimination continued and even grew. For that matter, all other legal distinctions between persons of different races tended to disappear. And in practice at least there was a general blurring of the divisory lines. The castas were no longer burdened with formal disabilities and disappeared as a category, and parish priests ceased the practice of recording information regarding race at baptisms and marriages. The war itself had encouraged the rise of mestizos and mulattos who had military talent; the shortage of Creole officers meant that many got promoted. And since soldiers and officers were often paid off in land, a powerful symbol of status, some of them or their descendants even entered the upper class. But these were examples of individual mobility, not the result of an altered social structure. Indeed, in most countries the confiscated estates of royalists ended up in the hands of the already wealthy, with the result that the concentration of landownership intensified. Finally, it is doubtful that significant changes occurred in the status of women directly as a result of independence, although much research still remains to be done on this matter. The civil codes drawn up by the newly independent republics tended to perpetuate colonial law on the family (which was generally more favorable to women than that in Britain and the United States), but the Napoleonic Code, which emphasized patriarchy, was widely admired and had some influence.

Instability and the Caudillo

Independence also meant the end of a government long considered legitimate in Spanish America. This result was perhaps the most obvious one, yet at the same time it was of the most profound significance. In fifteen years the insurgents swept aside a government that had ruled virtually unchallenged for three hundred. During all this earlier time there had been no coups d'état and no barracks revolts. Despite the latent anarchy which had characterized political life, the fact is that no one had seriously questioned the right of kings to rule or the right of the Bourbons and Braganzas to rule Latin America. And at the head of a corporate society, the sovereign's continued reign ensured the legitimacy of the entire structure. When he was gone, society was decapitated.

The result was like that of removing the flywheel of a machine. Moving at a faster and faster speed, it began to break up; bolts, nuts, springs, and gears flew in all directions. "This is chaos," wrote Bolívar. "Nothing can be done because the good people have disappeared and the bad ones have multiplied. . . . Everything is in a state of ferment and no men can be found for anything."[12] And for a long time in most countries of Spanish America rule by a dictator appeared to be the only alternative to anarchy. Forty revolutions occurred in Peru during the half century following San Martín's arrival, and eight different governments ruled there during 1834 alone. From the death of Bolívar to the end of the nineteenth century, Colombia had an average of one revolution per year and one constitution per decade. The events in Argentina during the wars of independence have already made this point clear. The temporary compromise worked out by Iturbide in 1821 between the divergent Mexican groups lasted only a few months; revolts and coups d'état dotted the country's subsequent history until 1854 while constitutions were regularly written, ignored, and rewritten. Throughout Latin America the basis of legitimate government—the acceptance of its right to rule by most of the ruled—had been destroyed by the wars of independence.

In some countries, perhaps luckier than Mexico, the age of chaos was more quickly succeeded by the rise of a strongman, or caudillo. Generally a military leader—either in the army (greatly enlarged by the independence wars) or at the head of irregular forces—he came to power by force and ruled as a dictator. But more than that, the caudillo exerted power through personal authority rather than through institutional means. He possessed charismatic qualities and could count on personal loyalties to maintain himself in power.

The caudillo was the result of social transition and not the evidence of social stagnation. In a perceptive study the historian Richard Morse argued that there are marked points of comparison between the postindependence politics of Latin America and the Age of Despots during the Italian Renaissance.[13] In both cases a long-established corporate society was seriously challenged. City-states or regions

---

[12] Quoted by Masur, *Simon Bolívar*, p. 437.

[13] Richard Morse, "Toward a Theory of Spanish American Government," *Journal of the History of Ideas*, 15 (1954), 71–93.

were carved out of a previously existing Christendom. Legitimate government thus disappeared. The religious underpinnings of the old regime were thrown into question. Just as the papacy had then been just one among many temporal powers, the Church now represented one of many competing forces or, as a spokesman for Spain, a foreign, hostile power. Into this crisis of legitimacy stepped the Prince or the caudillo. Without claim to legal power, he asserted himself by his dynamism, his personalism, his shrewdness. Like Savonarola, he may have been semimessianic in his appeal. In any case, he maintained his authority by guile and cunning and, as Morse puts it, "by proving his strength in life." He was as unscrupulous regarding the attainment of power as Machiavelli could have wished and sometimes as concerned for the welfare of his people as that writer urged.

The caudillo was not necessarily a landowner. Indeed, with notable exceptions such as Juan Manuel de Rosas of Argentina, it was probably more characteristic for him to be a landless mestizo, dissatisfied with his position and anxious to rise. With land in the hands of the aristocrats, mines owned by foreign investors, commercial activity increasingly controlled by foreigners too, and industrial prospects still nonexistent, the quickest way to change one's status was to control the government. This had already become a pattern during the wars of independence. Páez, a man of humble background, acquired immense properties as he became the major political figure of Venezuela until 1863.

If the caudillo rose by force, he generally fell by force, and, unless another caudillo was powerful enough to fill the breach, anarchy was the most usual outcome. Perhaps the only exception was Diego Portales (1797–1837) of Chile. Portales was no less a caudillo for being a successful businessman. He possessed both the qualities to attract loyalty and the strength of personality to enforce his will ruthlessly. He readily violated what the liberals called "individual rights"; exile or imprisonment was the fate of those who opposed him. In his private life he surrounded himself with well-dressed men and beautiful women. But to his machismo he added the qualities of a "perfect Prince." Not only was he genuinely concerned for the welfare of his country, he managed to institutionalize his power in such a way that stability lived after him. His secret seems to have been to involve the oligarchy directly in power rather than allowing them to observe political antics from afar. The army, for instance, was virtually replaced by a militia commanded by the landowners themselves.

Order and progress were the catchwords of Portales' regime. His police put down brigands, enabling entrepreneurs to develop heretofore untouched mineral resources. And conservative intellectuals produced a new constitution which called for an exceedingly strong executive power. This, Portales felt, was in keeping with the nature of his country at this time. As he had earlier put it, his ideal republic would have "a strong centralizing Government, whose members are genuine examples of virtue and patriotism, and [who] thus set the citizens on the straight path of order and the virtues."[14] According to this constitution, intendants were to carry out the president's will in the provinces, and the suspension of constitutional guarantees could be decreed by the president at almost any time. Although Portales was skeptical of paper constitutions, these ideas clearly reflected his views on ideal government. Eventually liberalism and democracy might have their place, but for now discipline and hierarchy were preferred. He restored the previously abolished entailed estates and raised property qualifications for voting. Portales held the common man in contempt and believed that the activity of irresponsible demagogues would destroy public tranquillity. Consequently, freedom of speech and press were curtailed. The end of the Spanish Empire had thus meant the end of a legitimate order that could be reconstructed only by returning, at least for the moment, to the hierarchical qualities of the colonial society, carefully entwining the interests of the state with those of the Creole oligarchy.

Such a painful search for legitimacy was almost unnecessary in Brazil, where the Braganza dynasty remained in power. Once a wing of that dynasty accepted its "Brazilianness" and came to terms with the Creoles, instability was eliminated and no caudillo found a vacuum of power in which to move. When, in 1831, Pedro I abdicated in behalf of his five-year-old son, Parliament chose regents to rule in his behalf. But this was as close as Brazil came to republicanism in those years. Even so, the centrifugal forces of regionalism and the breakdown of authority were so great that the boy was hastily

---

[14] Quoted by Simon Collier, *Ideas and Politics of Chilean Independence: 1808–1833* (Cambridge, Eng.: Cambridge University Press, 1967), p. 339.

crowned as soon as he turned fifteen. Subsequently, the regime preserved many of the characteristics of the corporate, hierarchical society in which the landed oligarchy found full opportunity to express its political will. So, if no caudillos emerged there, it was because Brazil refused to enter the transitional era in which old structures are violently broken up. When a brief period of caudillismo followed the overthrow of the emperor in 1889, the coffee planters organized their own militia and replaced army officers with one of their own as president, thus imitating in their own way the example of Chile.

If the crown in Brazil preserved legitimacy, it also prevented the pervasive regionalism of Latin America from forcing the creation of several nation-states. We have already noted the revolutions of 1817 and 1824 in northeastern Brazil, which proposed to create independent republics there. But the loyalty the Crown inspired in most Brazilians enabled the central government to put down these revolts and others that broke out before the new king was firmly in control. After 1849 Brazil enjoyed forty years of political stability. So it remained one country despite its distinct regions and immense size.

The rest of Latin America, lacking a king to secure the loyalties of diverse peoples, broke into many nations. The Viceroyalty of Río de la Plata became Uruguay, Paraguay, Argentina, and Bolivia; the Viceroyalty of New Granada became Colombia, Venezuela, and Ecuador; and the Viceroyalty of New Spain first became Mexico and the United Provinces of Central America, which then fragmented into five separate countries. The regional struggles that characterized the era of independence in Argentina were not put to rest until the high-minded caudillo Justo José de Urquiza managed, in 1862, to find a solution through compromise for the divergent regional interests. Chile probably had the most homogeneous society and the least divergent regions of any area in Spanish America, and yet it was also characterized by local rivalries that only strong government could keep in check. Likewise, a raging argument between federalists and centralists threatened at times to tear Mexico apart. There had not been a Mexican "nation" before independence, so the challenge here as elsewhere was to build a unity from divergent parts. Provincial leaders who had fought for home rule only gradually came to be persuaded that there were advantages to be gained from submitting to a strong central government. Here it must be emphasized once again that independence had always meant precisely local autonomy, loyalty to place.

Looking Ahead

The pace of change increased in the latter half of the nineteenth century under the leadership of a new generation. To begin with, these men were much more aware of the necessity of molding their liberalism to fit reality rather than the other way around. In addition, changing economic conditions led the rich to find some of the liberal programs acceptable. For instance, the transformation of Argentine agriculture now made it attractive to import immigrants to tend the prize beef herds, plant alfalfa, or raise wheat. Thus Domingo F. Sarmiento (1811–1888) was able during his tenure as president from 1868 to 1874 to institutionalize liberalism in Argentina. Its legitimacy now rested on the shared beliefs of the rural aristocracy and the urban elite. In Chile, too, moving cautiously and slowly, the liberals were able to gain power and carry out many of their most cherished reforms in such a way as not to threaten the landed oligarchy. Even in Brazil large advances toward a modern society were made particularly as a result of the growth of a new export economy based on coffee and the identification of new landowners with the forces of change.

But in Mexico years of anarchy seem to have precluded the softening of the conservatives, and more forthright measures had to be taken. Liberals there, hardened by their earlier defeats, successfully waged a violent civil war lasting from 1858 to 1860 in order to impose their program. It included the end of corporatively held land, severe restriction of the Church, and the final abolition of the fueros. When the conservatives turned to Napoleon III of France for support, offering the Mexican crown to the French-supported Archduke Maximilian, they unwittingly placed upon the liberals the mantle of national heroism. The French troops had to be recalled in 1867 to strengthen the French defenses against Germany, and the liberals quickly restored their power in Mexico.

But the liberal reforms continued to remove protective corporate institutions and expose the helpless to the raw competitive efforts of the better endowed. As the nineteenth century wore on, the mestizos and nonaristocratic middle elements of society tended to acquire enough power to move against the Indians in a feverish effort to milk from them the luxuries formerly enjoyed only by the upper classes. And the old Creoles, rather than restraining the mestizos as Spaniards had once restrained the Creoles, seemed satisfied to divert the aggressiveness of the mestizos away from themselves.

In the twentieth century one may discern an attempted synthesis of the colonial heritage and the nineteenth-century promise. The Mexican Revolution, which erupted with such force and violence in 1910, in some ways sought to restore the ancient protections for disadvantaged groups embodied in Spanish colonial law and to suggest corporate group rights alongside individual rights. It also challenged the notion of inviolable private property, whether in land or in subsoil mineral rights. By 1940 Mexican society was surely the socially most progressive in all of Latin America.

Other evidence of the synthesis can be found. We have noted that industrialization in Latin America generally advanced under close government supervision if not outright ownership reminiscent of Bourbon enlightened despotism. Sarmiento's easy willingness to admit the "inferiority" of the Spanish tradition was reversed by the self-conscious assertions of José Enrique Rodó (1872–1917), who, at the turn of this century, assured the youth of his native Uruguay that the Spanish heritage of spiritual, nonmaterialistic, transcendent values was worth more than a mess of industrialized Anglo-Saxon pottage. The surviving notion of a corporate society was given overt expression in the fascist-inspired constitutions of the 1930s. Still today the basic concepts of a corporate society underlie much of the ordinary Latin American's idea of government and the individual's relationship to it.

* * *

So if we ask: What resulted from the expansion of Europe? What were the effects in Latin America of the new Europe-directed economic system, the new Europe-minted ideology, and the new Europe-modeled style of life? the answers are anarchy, regionalism, the rise of the caudillo, and the exploitation of the poor. Or at least the combination of the colonial heritage with those outside forces had those results. And, if these forces destroyed the bases of political stability, only new sources of governmental legitimacy can restore them. It may be that only the pursuit of nationalism and social justice—two ideas also, ironically, strengthened by foreign examples—will provide the

Latin American governments the same degree of legitimacy as that enjoyed by the king in the older corporate society.

If closer ties with the wider world someday no longer mean maintaining Latin America on the periphery of an international economy that principally benefits the already developed countries but allows for genuine self-determination and real independence; if the ideology of freedom can eventually signify the fulfillment of the human potential not solely through individual struggle but also through cooperation and participation in community; and if the formerly oppressed gain an opportunity to join on a basis of equality in national decision making with full respect for human and political rights, then the processes that shaped the struggles examined in this book may be considered not only a major cause of Latin American difficulties but also the chief promise of its future peace and well-being.

Suggestions for Further Reading

Listed below are those books in English that I believe will be most useful to the reader interested in initiating a further study of the political independence of Latin America. Although the list is highly selective, there is a marked unevenness in quality among them because I have attempted to mention at least one on each major region. I have not included articles since the books below refer to the most provocative ones.

GENERAL

Bethell, Leslie, ed. *The Independence of Latin America*. Cambridge, Eng.: Cambridge University Press, 1987 [1985].

Domínguez, Jorge I. *Insurrection or Loyalty: The Breakdown of the Spanish American Empire*. Cambridge, Mass.: Harvard University Press, 1980.

Lynch, John. *The Spanish American Revolutions, 1808–1826*. New York: Norton, 1973.

BACKGROUND

Burkholder, Mark A., and Lyman L. Johnson. *Colonial Latin America*. New York: Oxford University Press, 1990.

Graham, Richard, ed. *Brazil and the World System*. Austin: University of Texas Press, 1991.

Herr, Richard. *An Historical Essay on Modern Spain*. Berkeley: University of California Press, 1971.

Lockhart, James, and Stuart B. Schwartz. *Early Latin America: A History of Colonial Spanish America and Brazil*. Cambridge, Eng.: Cambridge University Press, 1983.

Marques, A. H. Oliveira. *History of Portugal*. 2d ed. New York, 1976.

Maxwell, Kenneth R. *Conflicts and Conspiracies: Brazil and Portugal, 1750–1808*. Cambridge, Eng.: Cambridge University Press, 1973.

Prado Júnior, Caio. *The Colonial Background of Modern Brazil*. Trans. Suzette Macedo. Berkeley: University of California Press, 1967.

Savelle, Max. *Empires to Nations: Expansion in America, 1713–1824.* Minneapolis: University of Minnesota Press, 1974.

HAITI

James, C. L. R. *The Black Jacobins: Toussaint L'Ouverture and the San Domingo Revolution.* 2d ed. New York: Knopf, 1963.

Ott, Thomas O. *The Haitian Revolution, 1789–1804.* Knoxville: University of Tennessee Press, 1973.

MEXICO

Anna, Timothy E. *The Fall of the Royal Government in Mexico.* Lincoln, Neb.: University of Nebraska Press, 1978.

Detweiler, Robert, and Ramón Ruíz, eds. *Liberation in the Americas: Comparative Aspects of the Independence Movements in Mexico and the United States.* San Diego, Calif.: Campanile/San Diego State University, 1978.

Hamill, Hugh M., Jr. *The Hidalgo Revolt: Prelude to Mexican Independence.* Gainesville: University of Florida Press, 1966.

Hamnett, Brian R. *Roots of Insurgency: Mexican Regions, 1750–1824.* Cambridge, Eng.: Cambridge University Press, 1986.

Ladd, Doris M. *The Mexican Nobility at Independence, 1780–1826.* Austin: University of Texas at Austin—Institute of Latin American Studies, 1976.

Lindley, Richard B. *Haciendas and Economic Development: Guadalajara, Mexico, at Independence.* Austin: University of Texas Press, 1983.

Timmons, Wilbert H. *Morelos: Priest, Soldier, Statesman of Mexico.* El Paso: Texas Western College Press, 1963.

CENTRAL AMERICA

Rodríguez, Mario. *The Cádiz Experiment in Central America, 1808 to 1826.* Berkeley: University of California Press, 1978.

Torres Rivas, Edelberto. *History and Society in Central America.* Trans. Douglass Sullivan-Gonzalez. Austin: University of Texas Press, 1993.

Woodward, Ralph Lee, Jr. *Class Privilege and Economic Development: The Consulado de Comercio of Guatemala, 1793–1871.* Chapel Hill: University of North Carolina Press, 1966.

VENEZUELA, COLOMBIA, AND ECUADOR

Bushnell, David, ed. *The Liberator, Simón Bolívar: Man and Image.* New York: Knopf, 1970.

Johnson, John J., and Doris M. Ladd. *Simón Bolívar and Spanish American Independence, 1783–1830.* Princeton: Van Nostrand, 1968.

Masur, Gerhard. *Simón Bolívar.* 2d ed. Albuquerque: University of New Mexico Press, 1969.

Robertson, William Spence. *The Life of Miranda*. 2 vols. 1929. Reprint. New York: Cooper Square, 1969.

ARGENTINA, URUGUAY, AND CHILE

Collier, Simon. *Ideas and Politics of Chilean Independence, 1808–1833*. Cambridge, Eng.: Cambridge University Press, 1967.

Halperín Donghi, Tulio. *Politics, Economics, and Society in Argentina in the Revolutionary Period*. Trans. Richard Southern. Cambridge, Eng.: Cambridge University Press, 1975.

Rojas, Ricardo. *San Martín, Knight of the Andes*. Trans. Herschell Brichell and Carlos Videla. Garden City, N.Y.: Doubleday, Doran, 1945.

Romero, José Luis. *A History of Argentine Political Thought*. Trans. Thomas F. McGann. Stanford: Stanford University Press, 1963.

Street, John. *Artigas and the Emancipation of Uruguay*. Cambridge, Eng.: Cambridge University Press, 1959.

PERU AND BOLIVIA

Anna, Timothy E. *The Fall of the Royal Government in Peru*. Lincoln, Neb.: University of Nebraska Press, 1979.

Arnade, Charles W. *The Emergence of the Republic of Bolivia*. Gainesville: University of Florida Press, 1957.

BRAZIL

Barman, Roderick J. *Brazil: The Forging of a Nation, 1798–1852*. Stanford: Stanford University Press, 1988.

Macaulay, Neill. *Dom Pedro: The Struggle for Liberty in Brazil and Portugal, 1798–1834*. Durham, N.C.: Duke University Press, 1986.

Russell-Wood, A. J. R., ed. *From Colony to Nation: Essays on the Independence of Brazil*. Baltimore: Johns Hopkins University Press, 1975.

FOREIGN INFLUENCES

Costeloe, Michael P. *Response to Revolution: Imperial Spain and the Spanish American Revolutions, 1810–1840*. Cambridge, Eng.: Cambridge University Press, 1986.

Kaufman, William W. *British Policy and the Independence of Latin America, 1804–1828*. New Haven, Yale University Press, 1951.

Robertson, William Spence. *France and Latin American Independence*. 1939. Reprint. New York: Octagon, 1967.

Whitaker, Arthur P. *The United States and the Independence of Latin America, 1800–1830*. Baltimore: Johns Hopkins University Press, 1941.

Chronology

1700	Bourbons replace the Hapsburgs on throne of Spain
1776	Viceroyalty of Río de la Plata established; commandancy-general created in northern Mexico
1778	Decree of "Free Trade" ends system of monopoly ports in Spanish America
1780–1781	Rebellion of Tupac Amaru in Peru defeated
1789	Portuguese crush conspiracy for independence in Brazil
1791	Slave revolt begins in Haiti
1804	Haiti wins independence
1806	Miranda attempts to free Venezuela; first British defeat in Buenos Aires
1807	Second British defeat in Buenos Aires; Napoleon invades Portugal; Portuguese court and government sail for Brazil
1808	Brazilian ports opened to British trade; Joseph Bonaparte usurps Spanish throne; Central Junta of Seville coordinates anti-French effort; Montevideo organizes junta loyal to Central Junta; Mexican viceroy attempts revolution
1809	Juntas formed in Bolivia and Ecuador are crushed
January 1810	Central Junta in Spain defeated and replaced by regency
April 1810	Venezuelan junta assumes power and deposes captain-general
May 1810*	Junta replaces viceroy in Argentina
July 1810*	Junta assumes power in Paraguay
July 1810	Junta takes over in Colombia
September 1810	Hidalgo launches revolt in Mexico; junta organizes government in Chile

---

* Dates when countries became finally independent of Spain.

1811	Venezuelan congress declares independence; Hidalgo captured and executed in Mexico; Carrera leads coup in Chile, closing national assembly; triumvirate named in Buenos Aires; United Provinces of New Granada founded; Artigas retreats from Uruguay under threat of Portuguese invasion
1812	Spanish constitution promulgated; Spanish forces crush first independence movement in Venezuela
1813	British army and Spanish guerrillas drive French from Spain; Artigas reinvades Uruguay
1814	Ferdinand VII restored to throne of Spain; insurgents occupy Montevideo; Spanish forces victorious in Chile
1815	Spanish capture and execute Morelos in Mexico; Bolívar pens Jamaica letter outlining his political philosophy
1816*	Spanish occupy Bogotá; Congress of Tucumán convenes in Argentina and declares independence; new viceroy arrives to pacify Mexico
1818*	San Martín decisively defeats Spanish forces in Chile
1819	Bolívar victorious at Boyacá
1820	Liberals revolt in Spain and Portugal; Iturbide unifies independence forces in Mexico with the Three Guarantees
April 1821	John VI leaves Brazil in hands of son, Pedro, and returns to Portugal
July 1821	San Martín takes over in Lima
August 1821*	Mexico becomes independent
July 1822*	Bolívar establishes independent Gran Colombia and decrees formal incorporation of Ecuador
September 1822*	Pedro I declares Brazil an independent empire
1823	Portuguese forces completely driven out of Brazil; Central America separates from Mexico
1824*	Battle of Ayacucho frees Peru
1825*	General Sucre liberates Bolivia
1828*	Uruguay wins independence from Brazil
1830	Bolívar dies; Gran Colombia breaks up into Ecuador, Colombia, and Venezuela
1831	Pedro I abdicates throne of Brazil to his infant, Brazilian-born son
1838*	Nicaragua, Honduras, and Costa Rica declare independence from Guatemala

Glossary

audiencia	A high council to the viceroy and a court of appeals in Spanish America.
cabildo	A municipal or county council in Spanish America.
cabildo abierto	An emergency meeting of leading townspeople to discuss measures to be taken at a time of crisis.
câmara	A municipal or county council in Portuguese America.
castas	Those who, although not Indians living in communal villages, nevertheless paid the tribute. Originally limited to free blacks, mulattos, and mestizos, the category eventually included acculturated Indians and excluded most mestizos.
caudillismo	The caudillo institution or the practice of having caudillos.
caudillo	A political leader who rules through force or charisma, not by virtue of election or hereditary right.
conquistador	A sixteenth-century Spanish conqueror of Indian civilizations.
Cortes or Côrtes	The Spanish or Portuguese parliament.
Creole	A person born in Spanish America of European descent who has no, at least theoretically, Indian or African ancestors. In this book the word is also used for a person born in Portuguese America.
entail	The legal practice of settling property inalienably on a person and his descendants.
fueros	The special rights and privileges, especially to a separate court, pertaining to guilds, the Church, military officers, and other corporate groups.
gaucho	A cowboy in southern South America, usually of mixed racial background.
hacendado	The owner of an hacienda.
hacienda	A large landed estate. The word is used in this book to signify more particularly the economically self-sufficient units that satisfied local rather than

	European demands for agricultural products and were characterized by social relations of authority-dependency between owner and worker.
intendant	A government administrator of a large area who reported on some matters directly to the king.
junta	A committee or board, especially one with political power.
limeño	A resident of Lima.
llanero	A cowboy on the llanos of Venezuela, usually of mixed racial background
llanos	The plains, especially in Venezuela and Mexico, usually identified with a cattle-raising economy.
mestizo	A person of mixed Indian and white ancestry.
mulatto	A person of mixed black and white ancestry.
pampas	The plains, especially in southern South America, usually identified with a cattle-raising economy.
pardo	A free mulatto.
peninsular	A person from the Iberian peninsula in contrast to those born in America.
peon	A debt slave on an hacienda.
plantation	A large landed estate. The word is used in this book to signify the economic unit that produced export crops for European consumption and were worked by black slaves or workers paid in cash who were only impersonally related to the owner.
porteño	An inhabitant of the port city of Buenos Aires.
viceroy	A direct representative in America of the Spanish or Portuguese kings who was the highest executive, legislative, and judicial officer in each viceroyalty.

Index

About the Author

Richard Graham is Frances Higginbotham Nalle Professor of History at the University of Texas at Austin. He received his Ph.D. from the University of Texas in 1961 and has taught at Cornell University and the University of Utah and, as a visiting professor, at Yale University, Dartmouth College, Brandeis University, the Unversidade de São Paulo, and the Universidade Federal Fluminense, the latter two in Brazil. He served as president of the Conference on Latin American History and editor of the *Hispanic American Historical Review*. He has authored or edited numerous books and articles. His most recent book is entitled *Patronage and Politics in Nineteenth-Century Brazil*. He is currently at work on a social history of the provisioning of Bahia, Brazil, 1785–1850.